Deluxe Chimp

Deluxe Chimp

José Octavio Velasco-Tejeda

Library of Congress Control Number:		2014914782
ISBN:	Hardcover	978-1-4633-9102-7
	Softcover	978-1-4633-9100-3
	eBook	978-1-4633-9101-0

This book was printed in the United States of America.

Rev. date: 20/10/2014

To order additional copies of this book, please contact:
Palibrio
1663 Liberty Drive
Suite 200
Bloomington, IN 47403
Toll Free from the U.S.A 877.407.5847
Toll Free from Mexico 01.800.288.2243
Toll Free from Spain 900.866.949
From other International locations +1.812.671.9757
Fax: 01.812.355.1576
orders@palibrio.com
663395

CONTENTS

This book is dedicated to my older brother Fernando, who died very young. He introduced me to good music. My whole life became benefited quite a bit from it. A great deal of my everyday happiness is closely related to listening.

Books written in English by the same author (soon available in Spanish):

Deluxe chimp
Indelible Mark

Books written in Spanish by the same author (soon available in English):

Anécdotas, Relatos y Notas Interesantes (Anecdotes, Stories and Interesting Concepts)

Science fiction novel written by same author: (soon available in English):

¿Quieres vivir, o pasas? (Do you want to live, or pass?)

Sparse throughout this book, there appear upper case phrases enclosed by parenthesis, such as: (DENNIS MEADOWS – ECONOMICS AND LIMITS TO GROWTH (3)), which indicate the name of a video that can (at present) be downloaded from YOUTUBE and viewed by means of either YOUTUBE or REAL PLAYER. If at the end of said phrase, there is a number enclosed by another parenthesis, i.e. (3), it indicates de number of related videos. These videos are pertinent to the subject-matter being presented, and are suggested to be viewed as they are mentioned within the text. These videos are examples, and/or explanations that may further clarify the referred issue. If you rather see them at some other time, the book content is nonetheless complete, but you surely might miss useful, intelligent and complementing material.

There are several videos referring to vital issues, such as: Limits to Growth, Overpopulation, Climate Change, Evolution, Peak Oil, 9/11, etc.

A complete list of said videos appear in appendix I.

INTRODUCTION

Having around 99% of the exact same genes as our close cousins the chimps, the conclusion that can be extracted here, is that as marvelous as Homo sapiens can be, "he is, *at most*, a *deluxe chimp*". The title of this book is "borrowed" from the very interesting book from Carl Sagan and Ann Druyan: "Shadows of Forgotten Ancestors", where at the end of page 401, it reads: "the possibility that we are "no more than" deluxe chimps…"

Should this fact encourage, permit or even justify the behavior that quite a few homo sapiens (?) exemplify during their lifetimes, allowing greed, hate and stupidity, to rule their lives? Or, we have continually failed miserably to utilize our intellect, the only feature that really separates ourselves, from the rest of the animal kingdom (at least in degree). Seems to me, that we humans ought to be very thankful to the enormous luck of having being born, especially with the capacity to utilize creatively our mind. In fact, what a better way to show gratefulness, that precisely performing at best our intelligence? Now, thankful to whom or what? Without doubt, thankful to the random events that run the universe, in other words: thankful to evolution and plain luck (THE APE THAT GOT LUCKY).

The current global dangers are of very diverse nature, and everyday much more pressing. We, deluxe chimps, have dedicated ourselves untiringly (conscientiously most of the time), in the tasks of destroying, or at least, in seriously damaging all existing ecological habitats. Some of these, possibly almost impossible to restitute. The Earth, the oceans, rivers, and atmosphere are being contaminated without mercy. Innumerable species of plants and animals have been extinguished by us. And the extinction is forever.

Without doubt, the most powerful nations that protect their avaricious multinational companies are the guiltiest, and therefore the most responsible. The developing nations, with totally different situations, are responsible for a different form of devastation, perhaps just a little bit less guilty, because often their devastation deals with survival pressures.

Nevertheless, most us, human beings are responsible, in greater or smaller degree in wasting, deteriorating or contaminating everything that we use.

The recent invasion of the U. S. to Iraq, confirms the intentions of the most powerful nation on earth. Counting on a totally out of proportion military force, all other Earth nations, are at the mercy of which this country decides, it is best for them. Other wars and invasions surely will take place soon, especially as the imminent result of peak oil progressing (THE POLITICAL MOTIVATIONS BEHIND THE ORCHESTRATION OF 9/11).

The possible duplication of world-wide population (¡13 Billion!), perhaps before the end of the XXI century, no doubt will produce the reality of the old Malthusians warnings with respect to the excessive growth of the population. Even without doubling almost surely, finally "the destiny will reach us". This is, in fact, the "mother" of all other problems.

Dangers of comets and asteroids, which have not been investigated thoroughly, caused by an inexplicable reduction of the exploration of space due to ignorant and corrupt politicians.

The difference between the very few powerful nations and the vast developing countries becomes more abysmal every day.

The problem of shortage of potable water has also worsened. Apart from oil, almost certainly, will come several water wars.

The global drug trafficking, not content with destroying lives by means of its products, has turned some streets of some cities into battlefields, not to mention their dominant presence in vast numbers, at all levels of governments, almost worldwide.

Nevertheless, the main pressing danger seems to be the global climatic change, since the consequences can abruptly and radically endanger our survival. Along with this frightening future, now the imminent peak oil scenario (temporarily "revitalized" by the nasty Canadian tar sands), could become the last nail in the coffin of the deluxe chimp civilization, at least, as we know it. (PAT MURPHY BEYOND SUSTAINABILITY (4)), (THE END OF SUBURBIA), (THE LONG EMERGENCY), (PEAK EVERYTHING).

These and other issues constitute a great list of problems (in reality, predicaments) that have to be corrected, or rather, minimized its consequences, in the very short term, integrally and worldwide, before it is too late, if is not too late already.

Another one of the areas of greater deterioration has been, the area of "entertainment". With very few exceptions, it does not seem to have limits; the stupidity level, degradation, monotony and terrible taste presented/displayed, in virtually all means of dissemination available, accepted, sponsored, and now demanded, by global audiences.

It is amazing that being the only considerable difference between the human beings, and the rest of the animals, being this, of course, our capacity to acquire and to improve intelligence, sadly it is grossly wasted. Since this industry has taken this deterioration in gradual form, being in addition extremely adaptable the human being, we have been prepared surely to receive and accept, all the "garbage of images and sounds", that damage our mental health, as surely as, fast food damage our physical health. If children and adolescents "have been bombed" since the fifties, by means of progressive harmful material, it is no surprise, that already the small children of these generations enjoy it. But said explicitly, it stinks.

Evidently, the governments of practically all nations of the world, ignore the drastic reduction of values of their citizens, do not move a finger, with respect to trying to recover the lost values. Apparently, the problem without solution, resides in the fact that, existing the globalized society, the control is absolute with respect to what must be liked, be seen and be heard.

By having absolute control, the most powerful mass media and newspapers worldwide, propagate garbage and/or lies to the quiet recipients of such "entertainment/news". As the brave and really patriotic architect Richard Gage, the founder of the extremely important, and fortunately rapidly growing movement *9/11 Truth* very aptly says: "If you do not read the newspapers, you are uninformed, if you read the newspapers, you are misinformed".

The era in which tribes like the Huns, Vikings, Moors, or other conglomerates could bring resurgence of values, for a long time has ceased to exist. Therefore, we citizens of virtually any nation are alone, that is to say; our governments, the great corporations, the monopolies of mass media, the industry of the entertainment, almost with certainty, will not exert the positive necessary changes, with the required intensity to revert the damage to continue coming. Rather a more negative atmosphere is to be expected, unless a rare unexpected change happens.

The main problem resides in that we have been "half-baked educated", we have learned to read, memorize data, and believe most everything the churches, teachers, politicians, mass media, certain illusory books, horoscopes, shamans, homeopaths, etc., but we were not taught to question the validity or truth of anything. We do not employ the "scientific method" approach, which is the only known tool yet discovered to reach the truth. The use of our intelligence is not promoted, but just the opposite. The power of skeptical thinking is not encouraged, rather the opposite is the trend. Thus, the beastly avalanche of words, propaganda, advertisement, sounds and images with which the mass media bombard us, in all nations, every day, at all hours, is accepted without complaint by the masses. "The schools prepare soldiers with rifles that shoot corks, leaving us at the mercy of the incessant shrapnel of words, of which we do not know its meaning, turning us into a too easy prey of our emotions, instead of being its masters by means of our intellect". This frightening thought appeared in *The Lost Tools of Learning* paper by Dorothy Sayers, of the very important series, *New Horizons for Learning* managed by Dee Dickinson.

Specifically, the damage that I have been talking about is that this "entertainment", for over sixty years, is based on the exaltation of our (R-complex) reptilian brain, and almost null attention to intelligence. It would seem to be, that the intention is to locate the human being, at the intellectual level of a chimpanzee or surely even lower. The business of the "entertainment", today is out of control, continuously presenting infinity of disastrous examples that corrode the mind of the population in general and particularly that of children and adolescents.

My recommendation is that each one of us, must become tremendously selective in several vital aspects such as:

a. Accepting harmful laws and policies (in many aspects) to us, the citizens emitted by our governments, i.e. the "Patriot Act" recently promoted by Bush in the U.S.

b. Accepting products that damage environment and/or, that cause physical damage to us of any kind.

c. Accepting the marketing campaigns, that the governments allow, in where the advertisements contain lies, or are exaggerated, and often are based on dirty tactics. This applies so much to products, as to political campaigns.

d. Accepting fashions, entertainment, publicity, etc. that literally insult our intelligence, and reduces the good taste, and the moral principles.

e. Accepting the continuous promotion of which the only thing that matters is "to have", forgetting completely the much more crucial "to be".

Countless scientists, personally or via scientific associations, environmentalist societies, and several books of sustained credibility, in particular, the book; *The Limit to Growth*, originated from a study by the Club of Rome, have sent an alert with respect to really serious problems, that could explode near half of the XXI century, but are already showing the severity of what is coming to us (DENNIS MEADOWS - ECONOMICS AND THE LIMITS OF GROWTH (3)).

I think to have found a "Relational Linkage", that can be effective for the improvement of intelligence. I want immediately to stress that this, like any other effective method, that allows us to obtain true surprising results, requires extensive efforts, tenacity, patience, dedication, and intense passion. I have total confidence on the effectiveness of said scheme, one of the main subjects of this book. How can I be so sure? By applying not one but two methods (or techniques), used and accepted world-wide, to measure the intelligence levels and to compare them against the intelligence level, that have the people who dominates the method proposed in this book.

The first method consists of the GMAT (Graduate Management Admission Test). It is important to mention that, this comparison does not refer to taking the people that dominates my suggested method, and test them with GMAT. Rather, the comparison is based in that by using my suggested method, these people could obtain intelligent results much more rapidity, and would allow them to solve much more complex relations in diverse areas (with the due specific training required), almost without mistakes, than a person who obtains the best results in the GMAT test.

The second method, consists of a similar comparison, this time against a method described in a paper: *Components of a well-developed program to develop good abilities of intelligence,* written by Dr. Arthur L. Costa. In this case, I show how my suggested method amply fulfills all the components suggested in this program.

The third method, the "Relational Linkage", will be presented ahead, at the propitious moment.

I feel that I had great luck in finding one of the most reasonable, specific, entertaining, and logical method to substantially increase the capacity to acquire much greater intelligence, that it is so indispensable to attenuate the serious predicaments already commented, which become much critical every day.

A long time ago, I realized (felt certain) that governments (almost) worldwide, are interested in maintaining a low level of intelligence (stupid) citizens, in order to easily manipulate the masses. But a theory (or to feel certain) is of no use without a "proof". Therefore, I decided to test it as follows: I personally delivered letters to twelve of the embassies of the most important nations of the world (I have the stamped copies). Presumably, also the most "educated" countries. In said letters, I requested an appointment, in order to present the specific method to significantly enhance the level of intelligence mainly of children and teenagers. The result of this "adventure" is narrated in a following chapter.

ONE

Immediate and short term dangers

"When the world is over-populated, then the only remedy is war"
Thomas Hobbes

"Imaginative Cartoon" # 1: "BEFORE THE WORLD". This cartoon contains six images. In the 1st, there is an egg. In the 2nd, a chicken cracks open the shell and looks forward. In the 3rd, the chicken turns to its left. On the 4th, the chicken turns to its right. In the 5th, the chicken takes the piece of cracked shell that he broke and brings it back in place. In the 6th, it is shown the whole egg again (the cracks are shown), the chicken could not stand to step out.

The warnings that deal with the great variety of immediate and short term dangers (in this XXI century), caused by us or by natural causes, that put in serious danger of survival ours species, are countless. This chapter presents some of the most serious.

These warnings have been presented during ecological world-wide encounters. Also, ecological associations like Greenpeace, continuously inform us, about the increase of destruction in forests, seas, lakes, species, etc. Daily, species of plants and animals are exterminated, and as it says the announcement of Greenpeace: "the extinction is forever".

Scientists, in several countries, insist continuously alerting us about the caused ecological damages daily, on all possible human and wild habitats, terrestrial, marine and atmospheric. Great part of these damages are irreversible or at least, its recovery would take tens to hundreds of years, or even more.

These transcendent news are consider by most people, like totally trivial events, without importance, and consider much more important, a gossip with respect to a cinematographic artist, or the result of a sports event.

They are not important to most governments (since one does not see that they take sufficient suitable measures) and even less important for the multinational companies (that cause this destruction). Most of the people who worry, can do nothing on the matter, except not to consume articles made by companies that produce harmful products, or that cause ecological damages, during the manufacturing of these products. We can try to convince our community and family members, in order to unite, and boycott them.

We can and must use *rationally* the necessary things without waste.

We can and must recycle all the recyclable.

We can and must take care not to pollute and to contaminate the minimum possible (for example, rational use of the vehicle, walking is the healthiest exercise that exists).

We can and must love nature. Who was the one to propose that we must *dominate* nature, aside from the bible? Very likely he must have been an avaricious industrialist without conscience. But let us remember, that within the bible, God indicates; "Let us make man in our image and let them have *dominion* over the fish of the sea, and over the fowl of the air, and over the cattle, and *over all the earth*, and over every creeping thing that crept upon the earth".

Let us consider cancer. A single cell begins to work in unsuitable form and "decides to dominate its nature", that is to say; its home, the body where it lives. In a very short time, this cell manages to dominate its nature, as much so, that it obtains his assignment to the 100%. The 100% of dominion is equivalent to the death of its host, and all of these cancer cells die as a consequence.

It seems to me, this to be a sufficiently dramatic explanatory analogy with respect to what the human beings are doing to nature. Why is it so difficult to visualize and/or to understand, the damage that we are causing? Being earth finite, we think that its capacity is infinite? Or simply, we go towards the collective suicide, like the cell of the previous example. Does not matter to us, to preserve our own species? At least, does not matter to us, even to preserve our closest relatives, such as: our children and grandchildren?

In similar form, almost any infection that is not taken care of, can destroy the nature that allows it to live. Do we, Homo sapiens, have to be so absurd, illogical and suicidal like the cancer or the infections?

We have allowed, and literally contributed to, that our species constitutes the worse "infection" than can produce our self-annihilation. This situation has taken us only decades, not even millennia, is it reasonable?

Thus, everything seems to indicate that the "most intelligent" (sapiens) being of the creation, the deluxe chimp, decides its self-destruction and to leave this wonderful planet in exhausted and contaminated form, so that probably the insects and "germs", stay as their only inhabitants.

Then, to what type of information do we pay attention? Only to the daily information, that normally is irrelevant, monotonous and stupid, or worse; crimes, natural disasters and political scandals, that people hear without the minimum analysis on its content.

GLOBAL WARMING

Until not too long ago, I considered that among the multitude of severe problems that we have caused to ourselves, the global climate change was the priority number one and of course that continues to be extremely serious, even without confirmed evidence, which exists, that we are causing the problem. Not acting immediately and decisively constitutes a very serious danger and a criminal behavior. There is a very complete study, presented by a physics teacher in YOUTUBE (no name given) which I very amply recommend (HOW IT ALL ENDS INDEX (8)). Said teacher explicitly permits anybody to do whatever the viewer choses with the referred videos, inclusive selling them, what he cares for, is for the dissemination of that valuable information. This series of videos are very entertaining and explicit, so you can learn a lot about the causes and recommendations that he provides. Among other things, he considers that if humans are not causing the problem (which we almost certainly are) and we do act, the worst thing that will happen is that money will be spend without need. BUT, if we are causing it, and do not take immediate and intense worldwide measures, the delay almost surely will be disastrous.

But now, what is becoming another very hard pressing preoccupation issue, turns out to be, Peak Oil for, at least, four motives:

1-.   The eventual scarceness of the more superficial oil will force the utilization of oil and coal of lesser quality which will worsen the climate change.

2-.   The oil wars are continuing and, no doubt, will get worse (nuclear?), due to the scarcity of the hydrocarbons.

3-. The invasion of Iraq due to the "mass destruction weapons" farce (not even slingshots were found), but utilized as a pretext for 9/11, that evidently and demonstrable it was an inside job, as it is clear from very many books and videos (several of them mentioned here and listed in Appendix I).

4-. The myth and complot of the "war on terror" invented by Bush, Cheney, et all, is allowing that tyrannical laws that have been proclaimed in the U.S. and England, etc.

5-. The tar sands of Canada and elsewhere, if utilized, will cause a *game over* scenario, for the earth, as explained by the NASA scientist James Hansen.

Water: The new conflict that will confront the world

How much water do we have? Of the total volume of water, 98% is salty and is contained in the oceans. The rest, that is, around 2% is potable water and almost all of it is stored in the polar caps of the Antártida, Greenland and underground water; the most accessible is concentrated in rivers, lakes and dams and represents the 0.007 of all the Earth water. Of this amount, 87% is used for agriculture. What leaves only 10% for human consumption, with a population which grows without limit.

Industrialized countries use and waste a lot of water, while poor countries have major limitations for access. The amount of water in the world is affected by the floods, droughts and a threat to long term caused by global warming, because it will directly influence water resources. However, not all the water extracted may be utilized, because about half is lost through evaporation and another quarter is contraindicated for human consumption because it is contaminated

Limits to Growth

Probably, the more forceful investigation study is the published document: *The human predicament*, some years ago by the Club *of Rome*. This club is non-lucrative, it is a private association formed by industrialists, scientists, and civil government employees. This document originated the publication of the book: *The Limits to Growth* under the supervision of Drs. Donella and Dennis L. Meadows and associates of the M.I.T. (Massachusetts Institute of Technology).

The main preoccupation of this book is about the capacity of our planet, to take care of the necessities and the way of life of the always increasing, world-wide population that uses in an irrational and accelerated form, the natural resources of our planet. It is causing every day an irreversible ecological deteriorations, that puts in serious danger the global ecological balance. The logic mistake here is to think that acquiring limitless growth is equal to well-being (DENNIS MEADOWS – ECONOMICS AND LIMITS TO GROWTH (3)).

The material compiled by said book, does not predict the end of the world. The technique employed is called *Dynamic Analysis of Systems*, which interrelates five variables, that is to say: rate and amount of growth of the world-wide population, rate of use and availability of natural reserves, growth of capital and industrial production, food production and increase of global contamination.

Being these variables able to be quantified by means of observation, hypothesis, or approach, and expressed by means of equations, they constitute an ideal data source to be fed to the computer.

In this way, any number of "runs" can be obtained and evaluated. It is important to notice that; since the relations between these variables are not necessarily linear, the obtained results, are not as obvious as could be expected, rather totally unexpected results are most feasible to appear.

In fact, some results indicate that several positive and negative factors of feedback, show that short time goals could not be reached, also, show factors that will produce negative effects several years later. This is the reason for which the studies were elaborated at that time, hoping that sufficient anticipation existed.

This study shows that the population and the global production cannot continue growing without limit, due to limiting factors such as the progressive exhaustion of resources, the possible increase in the rate of mortality, and the negative effects of the global environmental contamination.

The approximate time reference when this situation may happen, is around half of the XXI century. Therefore, we are not speaking about human beings of unknown future, we are speaking of the time at which our children and grandchildren, could be surrounded in a world-wide crisis of survival.

Therefore, it is clear that we do not have, nor we can delay the solution to these problems to the following generation, simply will be too much behind schedule. Said tacitly, it would be a serious criminal act.

The general conclusions presented by the M.I.T team are:

"1-. If all the tendencies continue equal with respect to; global growth of population, industrialization, and contamination of environment, food production and exhaustion of natural resources, this planet will reach its limits to growth, within the following one hundred years.

2-. *It sees possible to alter these tendencies and to establish a stable* condition, which could stay so, during a considerable time. This global balance can be designed in such a form, that each human being could satisfy his material necessities, and have an equal opportunity to develop his potential.

3-. If the human beings, decide to dedicate their efforts to this second alternative, the sooner they begin, the success possibilities will be far better."

The common basic component that promotes the fast reach of the limits to growth, turns out to be the mathematical concept of *exponential* growth (THE MOST IMPORTANT VIDEO YOU''LL EVER SEE (8 parts)), that can be visualized in terms of the period of duplication, in other words, the time that takes in duplicating a certain amount.

The following French riddle, illustrates this concept of exponential growth, in a very appropriate form, the apparent hasty appearance in which a pre-established limit is reached.

Imagine a pool in where it grows aquatic lily. Every day this plant duplicates its size. If the plant grows totally without control, in 30 days it will cover the pool completely, eliminating all other form of life.

For a while, the plant seems small, so you decide not to take action, until this covers half of the pool. When will happen this? By all means, in day 29, so it is left a single day to save the pool. I believe that this example is most evident, and allows us to visualize the urgency to take measures in time, with respect to reaching the limits to growth.

Another very important factor that explains why the limits to growth, are reached so quickly, is explained by means of the concept: "positive feedback". A positive feedback is the one that does not have some means to restrict its growth, in other words, it is a wild circuit. All the mentioned dangers above are positive feedback circuits.

The first edition of the book: *The Limits to Growth*, was published in 1972. The considered world-wide population for year 2000 was of seven billion inhabitants, it can be corroborated, that this was approximately the existing number.

According to my understanding, the super huge problem that has triggered all other huge problems, has been, and it is, the absolutely out of control population "explosion". This can be summarized basically as a *sign* conceptual error. Economists primarily, followed by politicians, multinationals, religions and people, in general, are told and they believe: that *more is better*. We have to keep growing without limit. Of course, there have been some thinkers, that have been able to foresee, the tremendous consequences, that this stupidity has caused, is causing, and will cause, in every epoch with worse consequences, that the previous one. Because the correct sign to choose was the *minus sign*. Less of everything, especially less human population, would have been *the correct option*, by all means.

One very good example, was provided early in 1920 by Margaret Sanger. From the book: *Visions of Technology*, by Richard Rhodes, as I understood her, she blames her own sex as, something as babies *manufacturers* (7.5 billion approximately to date), and therefore guilty of the human predicament, of the atrocious overpopulation growth. Also, of the lack of intelligence and foresight to prevent human suffering. As any other product, in our financial world, when the offer exceeds demand, the price automatically is lowered, and thus, human labor became very cheap and disposable. The degree of that fact is evident, as we learn the wages that are paid to workers in the third world, are absolutely to permit only survival at extreme suffering. I believe, that Mrs. Sanger was too rigid to her own genre. Why not put, *at least half of the blame, on the over testosteroned macho?*

Since the subject of growth of population has been mentioned, it is almost inevitable to remember the name of Malthus, who in 1798 predicted that given that the population grows exponentially (geometrically), whereas the food production grows linearly (arithmetically), "soon" serious world-wide starving will become inevitable.

From then on, each follower of Malthus presented its fatal updated predictions, which also turned out to be mistaken. Thus, Malthus and his followers turned out to be totally mistaken. Even nowadays, several economists insist indeed that the well-being of the people will be increased, due to the population growth.

There was another thinker in this line, who thought that the most important benefit that offers a population that grows, it is to offer, to a given economy, the amount of knowledge that contributes to. If some type of matter is exhausted, what is the worry? That fact, will encourage somebody, to look for a substitute. Let us analyze this declaration:

a.   If uranium is exhausted, it does not matter, if forests are exhausted, it does not matter, if the oceans are exhausted due to contamination, it does not matter, etc., the human talent, will discover substitutes to compensate these exhausted reserves.

In which type of mind can fit this affirmation? As very wisely, David Attenborough stated; "anybody that thinks that infinite growth can take place in a finite world, is either mad, or it is an economist". The natural resources have lasted nearly four billion years, and one could think that man can destroy these resources, in some few hundred years?

b. From where can we be positive that the human talent, without doubt, will be someday be able to invent, each substitute that becomes exhausted?

c. We cannot assume, outside of all reality, that a greater population, is equivalent to greater knowledge available, uniformly and reasonably distributed around the world. An increase of population will be constituted, in great measure, by not well fed, and uneducated human beings.

d. The principle of inertia, specifically, if it happens that we were mistaken in the calculation in this aspect (many scientists think that today is already too late), reverting the situation would take too much time, and at unimaginable cost. Is it intelligent to take this risk?

e. There is a natural axiom that says: "The best thing in excess, is harmful" and unfortunately, we human, not being the best thing of nature, but rather we are very harmful and destructive.

f. The fact that Malthus and their followers were mistaken several times, means that they _always_ will be mistaken? ¡Of course not! (JANE GOODALL – OVERPOPULATION IN THE DEVELOPING WORLD), (WORLD OVERPOPULATION AWARENESS), (THE HUMAN OVERPOPULATION CRISIS).

David Pimentel, a scientist of the University of Cornell, who has dedicated thirty years from his life, to the study of the Earth capacity, insists that already several very serious problems exist. He thinks, that the Earth capacity is sufficient for only two billion people, *in the long term.*

It is not the situation that we will produce less food, rather; that the increases in production, will be much less spectacular than in the past, and we are awaiting for other five billion individuals.

A clear example of overpopulation exist in Easter Island. In this island, human figures and their respective giant stone heads exist, but in this island, a single tree does not exist. The material used to make the posts necessary to raise the heads to its place, from where did it come from? The most reasonable explanation is, that the previous inhabitants were very successful, *for some time.* As much so, that they had sufficient time, to dedicate it, to the manufacture of giant heads. Also, they overpopulated the island and they destroyed the ecosystems totally, leaving miserable monuments that intrigue archaeologists. The islands can maintain much people, *temporarily,* at the cost of exhausting the ecosystems, by reducing its capacity, in the long run. And this applies to islands, as well as to planets, ours in particular. Malthus was mistaken, but not by the error by which it is known. Rather; he did not understand, *that for some time,* the population can exceed the capacity of Earth. Almost surely: "the destiny will catch upon us" as it reads the title of an old film.

Let us return now to the commentaries with respect to the book: *The Limits to Growth,* which contains several computer "runs", which analyze the obtained results, when the five mentioned variables are modified.

The inevitable conclusion is that; even considering optimistic values (in one of the runs, the amount of well-known resources was duplicated), one or several runaway factors will produce dramatic consequences, before the end of the XXI century. Even considering reserves limitless, the contamination will produce a sudden and drastic reduction in the population.

Therefore, the only logic, reasonable and realistic (although evidently extremely difficult to implement at global level) recommendation that was emitted by the MIT team, turns out to be: *a state of balance.*

Does this recommendation needs to surprise us? Everything that we know, has to remain in balance, so that it can exist. An example of an inanimate object, - our sun-, that remains in balance, due to the tremendous force (towards outside) of nuclear fission, and the brutal gravitational force (towards its center). An example of an animated being is conclusive: a human being is made up of some 30 trillion cells. What happens if only one of them, severely loses its state of balance? Cancer is the answer, a runway situation has developed.

The basic definition of global balance is: "the population and the capital must remain stable, and the trend forces to increase or to reduce them, must remain in a state of carefully controlled balance".

What criterion we must use to choose between the several possible options? The most important decision turns out to be: during how long, we wish to maintain the balanced state?

When a period of time is chosen, the sufficiently ample minimum requirements to maintain a global balance are:

"1-. That the capital and the population remain constant. The birth rate equal to the mortality rate, the rate of investment equal to the rate of depreciation.

2-. All factors and products; rate of birth, rate of mortality, investment and depreciation must be maintained, at a minimum level.

3-. The levels between the capital and the population are established according to the values of the society. This could deliberately be modified and be fit slowly in agreement with the technological developments.

This type of balance, does not mean the end of progress, "only" implies that the investment of capital and the population, are maintained within limits. By all means, nobody can predict if this new society would be better or even different from the existing one, nowadays. Nevertheless, it is possible that a society that frees itself of the severe mentioned problems, could conceivable count on more energy and imagination, to direct them to the solution of other problems. A society that favors innovation and technological development, a society based on equality and justice is more probable that it can reach the mentioned state of balance.

Thus, a very deep human change is needed to be able to survive. For the first time during our civilization, a dramatic change of feeling is indispensable if the human beings are going to continue populating the Earth. This required change, will be neither automatic, nor easy to obtain. Several drastic previous changes in social and economic matters are necessary, that will allow the courage to obtain a generalized change of values."

The information mentioned above, has been well-known during decades, contained in tens of documented books written by several specialists, who have not been taken seriously or plainly ignored. But, why could be this?

Could it be, that we have lost our conservation instinct? Some possibilities are; our governments pretend to work hard in the solution of the problems, but they really work for their aims, and its egoistic interests, that frequently result harmful for the community, and the environment. At the same time, the citizens egoistically dedicate themselves to solve their personal problems, and they do not realize, or they do not wish to take actions, with respect to crucial subjects of world-wide importance.

Another probable cause could be; that we perceive that the required changes are so drastic and costly, that people prefer a global catastrophe, instead of sacrificing his present life style.

Finally, a last attempt to explain the fatal human passivity could be that, we do not count on other socioeconomic models to test. In fact, today under the global scheme, as I personally believe that it is the triumph of global government, predicted in several books from the beginning of the XX century. One of this books: *The Protocols of the elders of Zion*, in its 24 protocols clearly delineates the necessary steps to form a globalized world, ruled by a world government. The certainty that it is a true document is hard to prove, nevertheless, most of its predictions seem to have occurred. Just a coincidence? But, you may say, there does not exist a global government (yet), but in fact, a global financial control is a reality, which can control governments, stock exchanges, cause devaluations, global crisis, absolute control of all media, 9/11's, etc. (ZEITGEIST, THE MOVIE, FINAL EDITION),

Regarding; *to be or to have*, I can state, with all certainty and truth, that I have never had envy of material things. That does not mean, that I don`t like them; when I see a beautiful house, or admire, let`s say a Porsche, passing my car at full speed, I think *momentarily*, "nice home or nice car to have" and that`s it, or in other words: *next*, and my "envy" ends right there. But, I also admittedly recognize, many times, where I feel real "good" envy when I think: "It is a pity that I did not turn out lucky enough to be a "giant" scientist such as James Clerk Maxwell, or Archimedes, etc. and referring to the musical aspect; a Carl Saunders, a Chet Baker, a Bill Holman or a Bob Florence, to mention just a few.

Marketing

I consider marketing as one of the greatest evils of our time. In one occasion, a friend of mine commented that he had attended a marketing course, where the instructor mentioned that; "marketing is based on truth, because people are not stupid". If, in something marketing is not based upon, is in truth. At most, it is based, in "half truths". The only truth about marketing is; that it lies, exaggerates, deceives, and takes advantage of the naive, ignorant and good faith of the consumers. Secondly, no doubt that a great amount of people is stupid (or at least, uneducated), or how can we call millions of people, that believe blindly in superstition, horoscopes and homeopathy.

Even worse, marketing studies all, and each one of the human weaknesses, and based on this, it launches its marketing campaigns. Everything seems to indicate, that its fundamental intention consists in, turning stupid more and more people, so that then they can manage to deceive, so that their campaigns are less and less analyzed by us, and thus their deliberate deceptive ads become successful. Please take a big new box containing cereal (or many other products), for example. How much empty space is there in the upper part of the referred box? Why the box is not the exact size of the product there contained? Is this not a flagrant deceive to the consumer, allowed by governments? You bet.

Another example: a liquor company displayed in a "spectacular" ad in several important avenues in Mexico City. In this particular ad, it appears the face of an alert young man, not one who has been ingesting alcohol. What is the ad implying? Clearly, that by ingesting alcohol it turns you into a more receptive being. When analyzing this ad, I think that the displayed face, is the one of the man *before* it starts to ingest alcohol, not after. In the ad appears the question: WHAT MOVES YOU?, in great letters and an enormous vertical bottle covering his nose (in the middle of the eyes), that is to say, right in front and next to his brain. I want to clarify that I am not against "rationally" ingesting alcohol. I do it myself. The dangerous and harmful thing of this ad, is the *malevolent approach* that it projects, as always, specially directed for inexpert and easily malleable youth. Inevitable the direct implication that promotes is: "drink so that you can be moved ("to be successful", *in any area*) you inevitably are required to ingest alcohol, the more the better. Some recommendation to our youth.

¡Congratulations to one soda pop manufacturer for a spectacular ad! You are the proud employer of a very bright "creative", as it can be seen in a past ad posted in Mexico City that read; "For every bad news, there are five mothers expecting a baby". Doesn't this guy realize the stupidity that he is announcing? The manager of this guy doesn't either? How about the regional manager, the international manager and the CEO? None of them, up to the highest position? Haven`t anyone of them, read about yet the high probability that the world population will reach the 13 billion mark, before the end of this century? That is, if we are still around. But, of course, soda pops, for so many people, are wonderful. That is, for you, what really matters. Also congratulations regarding your lobbing effort which eliminated the prohibition to sell junk food at schools, that will allow you to accumulate more billions of dollars. For you, the end (greed) justify the means (diabetes, obesity, etc.).

One of the ads that seem more aberrant, by its obtuse cynicism is the one that states "Xvisión, Intelligent, like you". If something *is not* intelligent (except for the rarest exceptions), are the contents that are presented in this wonderful apparatus that could promote true civilization, and that its persistence, for many years, has been to degrade and to stultify, to the maximum possible audience. When it seems to be that no longer something more aberrant and vulgar can exist, something much worse arise.

I understand that in our world, marketing is inevitable, desirable and even essential, in which I do not agree absolutely, is in the *approach* presented, based on hair-splitting lies, vulgarity, excess, half-truths and deceits directed to all levels, and yes, sex presented in the more vulgar possible way. Also, the compulsion it creates to buy, like there in no tomorrow (which might come true).

Entertainment

"Imaginative Cartoon # 2". In this caricature, we observe a TV sitting comfortably in its chair, it has a remote control in its hand pointing at a table where it appears... a brain. More descriptive, impossible.

Global movement against truth and beauty.

I wonder why I am one of the few who disapproves ads, most sports, movies, TV, and modern "music"? We have too much, too repetitively, at high volume and there is no silence at home, store, shopping mall, transportation, or restaurant (DON HAROLD SILENCE). I feel overwhelmed with such disgrace. Our actual "civilization", has become totally oblivious of the existence of truth and beauty. What astounds me, is that the rest of the people is completely at ease, with this monstrous transformation. It has to be planned, I do not believe it to be circumstantial. That way, you do not have the time and the appropriate environment to think, that simple. The really important matters are evaded. The important subject is; who won yesterday's tennis game, not the Peak Oil emergency. In addition politics stink, and politicians are very corrupt (with a few exceptions). Had Homo sapiens chosen truth and beauty, as one of the golden rules to follow, a complete different civilization would be our habitat, and the legacy to our children and grandchildren. When you think sometimes that the bottom of vileness, vulgarity, violence, absurdity, monotony, etc., has finally arrived, someone will be able to invent something even worse.

With respect to the movies and TV, the avidity with which global audience is so expectant, or better said, addict, ignore the alarming intellectual damage that they cause. Not only is generalized violence to the maximum degree. The language utilized is most despicable, so repetitive, unnecessary, and with total lack of taste. These aspects are really the "universities" where the equivalent of a degree majoring in: "What not ever to do", could be attained. Many years ago, when I attended to the cinema, I went to watch "recommended" pictures mostly, where I became dumbfounded by the scenes and language projected. When I later commented to the person that proposed said recommendation, the answer was always: "¡Then you did not understand the message of the picture!". The norm therefore is; ignore all the very grotesque, violent, nasty, immoral, vulgar, monotonous aspect, etc., and concentrate only in the final part, !see only how happy the family reunited at the end¡, disregard all the revolting nasty happenings during the plot. So, assuming there is a "message" to consider, should I tolerate two hours of idiocy, or whatever its duration takes?

A well-known comedian commented; "If all rude words said in current pictures were removed, we would be back to silent films".

Nowadays, the "successes" of the cinema, the television and "music" are extraordinary. I am speaking of its economic aspect solely. It is truly impressive to see audiences formed by several thousand fanatics, which previously have been conditioned to receive garbage, without artistic, creative, educative and moral content.

Nowadays, most everybody accept, whatever the mass media decides to broadcast. They receive, nobody questions, or complain about its total lack of quality.

If an extraterrestrial astronaut analyzed all the daily TV programming, of the entertaining media in general, he would correctly deduce that we terrestrial beings count with excellent means, *if what we want,is to teach* the population how to commit atrocities, barbaric behavior, lies, treasons, murders, crimes, violence, acts of infidelity, etc., that is to say; any type of attitude that does not imply, not even remotely, the use of intelligence, values, moral, not even common sense.

Let us analyze what happens when people consume fast food. In the first place, they get used to eating frequently this garbage and secondly they end up liking it. Rapidly, they will become increasingly obese, they do not realize and/or it does not matter to them, that their body looks so bad, and still worse, that their organism maintains internally high cholesterol, triglycerides, uric acid, etc. Not in vain, the first cause of death in the first world countries, is the heart attack.

Now, if this happens to the body caused due to this kind of "food", what happens to our mind when we take junk entertainment of any kind? Something very similar, but this time the attack is nothing less that, against our brain. The majority of the modern entertainment, contains such amount of truly harmful junk for our more appraised treasure, our brain, that the result is evident, when we find out the news around the world.

The globalization of the brutality, the stupidity, the bad education, and terrible examples, etc. it is not by chance, it is the daily result of the lessons of mass entertainment starting from before birth, that will produce on them: "cerebral cholesterol" (stupidity).

Like intelligent beings that we supposedly are, we do not have to continue tolerating the destructive type of present entertainment. Let us remember, the scarce genetic and social margin that separates us from our cousins the chimpanzees. Let us tend to models like, for example; Leonardo Da Vinci, not towards a macaque.

Dangers of impacts of comets and asteroids.

It is amazing that life exists on earth. The thickness of the volume where it is possible is confined to the terrestrial surface and a few kilometers above and below sea level. Outside that very limited volume, the universe, is an absolutely inhospitable place, in all aspects.

One of the ever present dangers to our planet, is the presence of comets and asteroids, that eventually cross the earth orbit. This fact, has been demonstrated by the extinction of species, that have been studied by geologists, that have found sediments of iridium, a very rare metal on earth, but very common in asteroids. The most clear evidence of impacts are found in the Arizona crater, and the one found in Yucatan.

The amount of comets and asteroids that continuously cross terrestrial orbits and the verification of past collisions against the Earth, moon, Jupiter and almost any celestial body that we have studied, presents tremendous restlessness to us, not if we will get hit or not, but rather *when* the following impact will take place, and of which magnitude it will be.

Thanks mainly to the warnings and studies of the scientists Shoemaker, finally some governments have begun to worry, with respect to the destruction that can cause the impact of a comet or an asteroid, to the Earth.

At present, an organization of astronomers exists who are watching threatening celestial bodies, with size of 1 km or greater, nevertheless, given that the possibility of an impact, is quite greater compared with the possibility of a passenger involved in a commercial flight accident, it is vital that dedication to this risk should be more intense. It is worth the trouble, and its cost. The most dramatic example of the damage that can cause an impact is the one that caused the extinction of the dinosaurs (and very many other species) some 65 million years ago. Everything seems to indicate that the crater produced by this impact, is in Yucatan, México. The corresponding study to this important event was carried out by doctors Luis and Walter Alvarez (father and son), where they found ample evidence that the tremendous impact occurred in that place.

Why bodies of "only" 1 km in length or greater, are considered really dangerous for the civilization, and therefore they are the unique ones, to which it is worthwhile to watch? Why, a small body, compared with the size of the Earth, can cause so much damage? The answer is the enormous speed at which they travel, that is of the order of: 60,000 Km/seg. The damage caused by the impact, can be equivalent to the explosion of the existing arsenal of atomic bombs, whose effect is to produce trillions of tons of dust, which would surround the Earth, preventing the passage of solar light, for many months. The result would be the death of all vegetables, by the impossibility to produce photosynthesis. This fact, quickly would be followed by the death of the vegetarian animals, and in consequence the death of the greater predators. If the impact would take place in the sea, a resulting tsunami, would produce waves 100 meters high anywhere in the world, with the corresponding destruction to cities.

Frequently, we know of relatively small asteroids, able to destroy at least a great city, that cross the Earth trajectory, which have missed impact by a few hours. Although really space is so plentiful, there exist such amount of comets and asteroids that, rather often appear dangerous situations, as for example the spectacular crash of several fragments of a comet that hit Jupiter in 1993. That divided comet discovered by the astronomers Shoemaker (husband and wife) and

Levy, confirm the existing real danger. Each fragment produced an approximate impact area as large as the Earth. That is to say, had they not been attracted by Jupiter, very likely, they would have hit the Earth, probably not even the insects could survive. Therefore, it is urgent that the space activity, and interplanetary trips start again (although, without oil, very likely it will not be possible any more).

PEAK OIL

Like all other extremely severe predicaments that face humanity during the decade of 2010, peak oil (RICHARD HEIBERG PEAK OIL) (MATT SIMMONS PEAK OIL) (PAT MURPHY PEAK OIL) (COLIN CAMPBELL, PEAK OIL) (MIKE RUPERT PEAK OIL & COLLAPSE) (DR, PETER LLOYD PEAK OIL) is bluntly ignored by governments, industry, economists, politicians, and the general population. The consequences of such inaction, will probably cause the end of civilization (at least, as we know it). Instead of modifying our very wasteful way of living, in an orderly pace, we are permitting that the impact becomes a time bomb. In fact, this coming catastrophe is amplified, because the depletion of most natural resources, is also coming to an end (RICHARD HEIMBERG PEAK EVERYTHING (6)). One of the most important books in this vital issue is; *The Party is Over,* by Richard Heinberg where he explains that peak oil appears whenever the maximum oil extraction starts to decline, following a bell shaped curve. At that point; no known technology, will ever allow production to increase again, at a reasonable price. Also; the quality of the oil thereafter extracted, will deteriorate very rapidly. That is true for the extraction of a well, a field, a state, a nation and worldwide.

The implications are enormous. Actual agriculture requires vast amounts of oil and gas derivatives for pesticides, fertilizers and diesel for powering machinery. The transportation of all that food, is required to be moved for very long distances, to replenish supermarkets, consuming great quantities of gasoline. Millions of automobiles, requiring millions of gallons of gasoline daily for suburbs commuting, will be unable to circulate (THE END OF SUBURBIA) (THE LONG EMERGENCY). Just imagine that you (and everybody else) find; "out of gas" signs posted in every gas station in your neighborhood, your county, your state, the whole nation? Wars will follow: in fact, the wars in Afghanistan and Iraq are oil wars (RICHARD HEINBERG THE POLITICAL MOTIVATIONS BEHIND THE ORCHESTRATION OF 9/11).

Due to the fact, that the better grade hydrocarbons will soon be all gone, aside from the higher price, the pollution level will increase because, lower grade combustibles contain much more contaminants, such as sulfur.

Am I trying to scare you? You bet. I am very scared myself, not for myself, since I am 76 years old, but very much so, for the future of my children and grandchildren (not to mention our species). But how about directing our preoccupation to a very conscious occupation, that could somehow reduce the coming suffering by the following suggestions to assume ASAP:

1-. Learn Perm culture, and apply it in whatever area you have, it takes a lot of time to become acquainted with it.

2-. Get out of debt.

3-. Spread the word and get together with your community with the purpose of forming a "Post-carbon" community.

4-. Walk and use bicycle and much less your car, whenever possible.

5-. Be informed, regarding the current outcome with related topics.

6-. Learn "old trades" they will be very useful and needed, in the near future.

7-. Keep or buy and/or manufacture if possible, any type of manual (non powered) tools. People will need to get such tools.

8-. Do not waste anything (energy, food, water, etc.) and recycle everything you can.

We can see that our predicament is really astounding, any one of the dangers here presented, is by itself, worth of very special attention and immediate response, but with all probability the consequences of peak oil, will be the final blow that will produce devastating global disasters of all types.

SEPTEMBER 11, 2001

The examples of the deceits of the governments are countless; as a recent example of this immoral performance, we have the invasion of Iraq, where there was not the slightest evidence of the massive destruction arms, that Bush and Blair were so confident to find. Truth coming to light revealed that; with base in lies, Bush convinced Congress, and Blair the House of Commons, so that they supported the invasion. The true intention was and is, the control of petroleum (among other economic reasons). With this aggression without precedent, the era of "preventive" invasions of the great powers has begun. They demonstrated that the importance that the initiatives of the United Nations have, is inexistent, which questions the reason of being of this expensive institution.

Since I have written some other related important text in another of my books: *(Anecdotes, Stories and Interesting Concepts)*, because includes a color picture (this book have none) and last, not to become repetitive, I will only mention that I volunteered to help the 9/11 Truth Movement, doing translation (English-Spanish) of four scientific papers, related to the analysis of the details of the destruction of the towers, and one translation of a conference by Richard Gage, which were published. The related picture is a "spectacular" ad, placed exactly at one corner of Times Square in New York, which lasted posted several months, starting on September of last year, to commemorate the 12th. anniversary of that horrendous crime. The content of said ad, is basically this: Did you know that a ***third*** building was blown down (by controlled demolition, exactly as the other two) on September 11? Very few people know this, *because the live coverage was transmitted only that terrible day*! No more repetitions of that event were ever transmitted again. I almost got selected for coordinating the posting of similar ads in Mexico City, but sadly the budget had to be drastically reduced. Many other cities were also affected. I tried two radio stations to report about that event but no response was received, let alone the mentioning of that event. It appears to be total control, of what can be *aired* and what not.

There exist several videos in Internet regarding the "Mickey Mouse" level "investigation", where remain multitude of unanswered questions. But the mounting evidence, points straight to a very poorly staged inside job. Inconceivably, but similar to many transcendental worldwide events, in addition to 9-11, such as Kennedy's assassinations (three members of said family), remain obscure in spite to thinking groups that "demand" the questions to be resolved at a mature level. Governments might get away fooling millions, but there also exist a good number of people that are not stupid. The complete set of 9-11 proofs, are too ample to be included in this book, but I will include some of the most conclusive as follows: (EVIDENCE THAT GEORGE W. BUSH HAD ADVANCED KNOWLEDGE), (SCHOLARS FOR 9/11 THRUTH), (9/11 TOTAL PROOF THAT BOMBS WERE PLACED IN THE BUILDINGS) and many more videos.

If you can compare, and I mention this, *because, if you would*, 100% of the intelligent people of the world would have certainty of what happened, even if they do not have, the remotest idea of engineering. Let's ponder this; has **_ever_** a building been *destroyed*, as did the two twin towers **in addition to "building 7"**, which was not even hit by a plane and "coincidentally", contained all the conviction documentation referring to the huge fraud of ENRON, and other many fraudulent companies. The *three* huge buildings **_exploded_** in **_almost identical form_**, in less than twelve hours? Does it not, terrible earthquakes affecting us, so often, that produce energy millions of times more destructive than an airliner? However **never, even remotely**, the collapsed building resembles, in the least, the aforementioned *destructions*. But now, compare **any** building which has been **_destroyed, by the way_**, of: **_"controlled explosive demolition"_**. It is clear and virtually identical regarding: free-fall time (WTC7: NIST FINALLY ADMITS FREE FALL (PART 1)), huge clouds of powdered cement and other materials, vertical drop on their own footprints, no floor over floor, since everything got vaporized and pulverized, sounds of explosions substantiated by multiple witnesses (including firefighters who were on those sites), (9/11 FIREFIGHTERS REVEAL HUGE EXPLOSIONS BEFORE TOWERS) etc. etc. etc., *__and of course, the "lakes" of cast iron in their foundations that lasted weeks to cool down, and also residues of the most powerful known explosive waste__*. (9-11 CONSPIRACY: NIST CHEEF ENGINEER LIES ABOUT MOLTEN METAL), and many, many more.

Add to this the; "report on the *__start__* of the collapse" and there stop its findings, ¡close to 10,000 printed sheets, to stop there!, by the Agency that "investigated" the causes (NIST). The report is full of inconsistencies, omissions, errors, lacking in analysis of the causes (virtually all steel, very conveniently, had the appropriate size for its very rapid "disappearance", which was quickly removed from the scene of the crime, and sent to China). *__This, gives you a slight idea of what governments can cause to the world, even to their own country and citizens__*. **Because not even happy with such atrocity, which has no name that defines it properly, they have __threatened with worse things that will happen. Because, if they are the perpetrators, surely they know!__**

The main problem is that for the buildings to have come straight down, "All 287 columns would have to have weakened to the point of collapse at almost the same instant."

Features of Controlled Demolitions

The vivid, redundant evidence of numerous features of controlled demolitions in the destruction of the Twin Towers, is the basis for a simple, persuasive, inductive argument, for the involvement of controlled demolition. Dr. David Ray Griffin provided a concise list of ten features of controlled demolition, exhibited in the destruction of WTC 1, 2, and 7 in: *Omissions and Distortions*:

1. Each collapse occurred at virtually free fall speed.
2. Each building collapsed straight down, for the most part, onto its own footprint.[11]
3. Virtually all the concrete was turned into very fine dust.
4. In the case of the Twin Towers, the dust was blown out horizontally for 200 feet or more.[12]
5. The collapses were total, leaving no steel columns sticking up hundreds of feet into the air.
6. Videos of the collapses reveal "demolition waves", meaning "confluent rows of small explosions."[13]
7. Most of the steel beams and columns came down in sections that were no more than 30 feet long.[14]
8. According to many witnesses, explosions occurred within the buildings.[15]
9. Each collapse was associated with detectable seismic vibrations (suggestive of underground explosions).
10. Each collapse produced molten steel (which would be produced by explosives), resulting in "hot spots", that remained for months."

I recently found two very interesting videos (RETIRED EXPERT PILOT JOHN LEAR- NO PLANES HIT THE TOWERS), (THE BEST 9/11 DOCUMENTARY) where it is explained conclusively that no planes were used, all the "show" was done in computer simulations. This is otherwise evident, since no plane can go through a massive building intact, without leaving not even a single screw or rivet behind, except that in case of the first tower, that was (supposedly) hit, a jet engine was found on Murray street, unfortunately, or fortunately, it was an engine not corresponding to a Boeing 767 (this important evidence, was also "vanished", which is another criminal offense). Of all the videos of evidence that I keep, I do not recall even one of them, showing the jet engine, as shown in these videos, just mentioned above. The viewing of the referred jet engine, triggered a memory of a document, that mentioned said motor, a long time ago. So, I went searching my binders, and sure enough, I had filed a letter sent by a cousin, −a survivor−, on September 16, 2001. He narrates that; while coming out of the subway, on City Hall Park, he realized that something bad had occurred, because a large amount of people was going the opposite way, being this a rush-hour moment. When entering Murray St., he was surprised to find *a jet engine*, laying on the crosswalk, almost in front of where his office was, and he proceeded to enter the building. A few minutes later, a tremendous deafening roar was heard, and an earthquake was felt. He tried to escape, but when opening the door, a compact cloud of dust and debris, made it impossible to breathe and see, so he closed the door, in a hurry. After a few more minutes, he tried again, and almost frozen to death, by fear, he decided to run for his life. When he was outdoors, it was possible to see, what had caused all the noise and shattering was due, to the collapsing of the North Tower. He, as well as, hundreds of persons, were running to save their lives. Fortunately, my cousin was able to escape from death, which was planned and executed by his own government.

One of the events that I would like to see before I die, is that the ever growing 9-11 Truth movement, succeeds in achieving a new independent investigation, where the traitors (top level government agencies, laboratories, media, etc.) are judged and convicted for the crimes they perpetuated (KATHY MCGRADE B.S. METALLURGICAL ENGINEER), (9-11 BLUEPRINT FOR TRUTH (13)).

Civilization Types

As appears in internet: the classification that the Russian astronomer Nikolai Kardashev has on the degree of technological advance of a civilization, as follows:

A civilization type I, is that one that controls the whole planet. They can control the climate, prevent earthquakes… They have already finished the exploration of the Solar System.

A civilization type II, is that one that controls the energy of the sun. The requirements of energy of this civilization are so great, that it directly consumes the energy of the sun, to move his machines. This civilization has initiated the colonization of local star systems.

A civilization type III, is that one that controls the energy of a complete galaxy. It controls the energy of thousands of million star systems. Probably already dominates Einstein equations and it can manipulate space-time at will.

Our civilization, however, is type 0, it is initiating space travel and consuming fossils fuels. It is very worrisome how we are very quickly damaging the ecology of the planet, and at this pace, we will not be able to aspire to obtain a change of category, we could not survive much longer.

TWO

ONLY FORSEEABLE POTENTIAL SOLUTION

"Crowds have lots of heads but little brains"
Thomas Fuller

"Imaginative cartoon # 3". In this cartoon, appears the late scientist Albert Einstein in front of a blackboard, where he has written: $E=ma^2$, which has been crossed out. Below that equation, there is a new equation, this time: $E=mb^2$, which has been also crossed out, while Einstein, smoking his famous pipe, is trying to figure out what is wrong.

I believe, with great conviction, that the variety of problems (actually predicaments) mentioned in the previous chapter, additionally to the multitude of non-mentioned problems, and others that doubtlessly will appear, as time goes by, that they can only be "partially solved" by means of this attempted remedy. I consider that this integral "solution" consists, at least, of the following parts: <u>knowledge and rational generalized application of science (not to mention quality education at all levels), generalized improvement of intelligence (and obviously, its wise utilization), generalized restitution of the lost moral values, and a drastic reduction of the difference of wealth between rich and poor countries, all this at world-wide level.</u>

Given our present situation, each one of these subjects, seems like very near to impossible. Maybe they are. But, if I believe to have "something", that could help revert, or at least attenuate, this sad world-wide situation, as difficult as it may seem, I consider presenting it in a book morally obligatory. Everything has conspired to arrive to the serious present deterioration. Governments, industry, great multinational corporations, the entertainment mass media, and practically all the inhabitants of this over-populated earth, to mention only some causes. So capable have been all these actors, at world-wide level, that educated and cultured people, have been forced to accepted this situation, and very few attempts have been made to fight them. We have not been able to construct a front-line defense and have decided to allow aggressions, of all types to our world, country and, in particular, to our intelligence.

Knowledge of science and its generalized application.

Science. What comfortable attitude exists towards science in the immense world-wide population. We use excessively, all the products that the technology, practical derivation of science, presents to us daily. The contamination and waste of the natural resources, while they satisfy our compulsion to consume, seems to us, all right. We do not consider the nasty problems that we will inherit to our children and grandchildren. We, do not want to worry now, we decide. That comfortable and avaricious attitude of the corporations, which have great laboratories, where the scientists make their discoveries. Comfortable because, very frequently, the products are not sufficiently tested, often they know the damage that they cause directly or indirectly, and even so, they send them to the market. Comfortable because the only thing that worries them, is to sell even more, at the cost of highly harmful contamination of all kinds. I am thinking, for example, in the so attractive but so polluting non-degradable packing.

Science turns out to be neither good nor bad, morally speaking. For example, the most serious threat produced by man until now, the atomic energy, used like bombs, can end civilization, but as a nuclear reactor can be used for the production of enormous amounts of energy for pacific use (unfortunately it is dangerous and it produces very dangerous, and lost lasting wastes), but that is another subject. That is to say, it is the use that we make of it, what could be described as good or bad.

Speaking of the atomic bomb, being the American physicist Robert Oppenhaimer, who was in charge of the Manhattan project (development of the atomic bomb), during a meeting with president Harry Truman, mentioned that "I think I have blood in my hands" (THE ATOMIC AGE ROBERT OPPENHAIMER) (SCIENCE AND THE SOUL: ROBERT J. OPPENHEIMER / DR. ATOM), talking about how the device was used. When the meeting was over. Truman called Dean Acheson and indicated him that he never wanted to see Oppenhaimer again. Truman even call Oppenheimer a "cry-baby". Here we see a sad scientist that recognized how badly science had been used and the politician directly responsible for its use, incapable of a minimum gesture of repentance or at least the acceptance of the terrible fact.

With respect to science, I think that we require *urgently:*

1 -.   At childhood stage. As for practically any activity that it is worth the trouble, that it is desired to appreciate, and

master during their lifetime, science would have to become accessible for all the children of the world. If we let time go by, it will be more difficult to make this proposal viable. This is confirmed by their own experience, the eminent scientists, Richard Feynman, Michio Kaku, etc. Given the immense curiosity of all children, it is indeed the proper time to interest them in science. Not an easy activity, if it is really desired to obtain "potential scientists", the improper indoctrination can result insufficiently interesting, it may not captivate their imagination and could cause that they would not want to continue investigating, or worse, they could even take aversion to this subject. It is indispensable to count with an immense body of highly trained teachers that have passion regarding their "subjects", and also have skillful teaching capacities.

2-.   The youth stage. If the awareness of science is started during childhood, or not, it is imperative that the learning of science continues (or initiates, in its case) in this stage of growth, adapted to the corresponding age. When I talk here about science, I speak of all the branches of science. Hopefully most of these branches of science are available, so that young people can choose the branch that attracts them most. It is desirable and possible that these small novice scientists, can develop polymath habits, that is to say, scientists that manage to be proficient in time, with several branches of science concurrently. It is very important to develop a great number of "generalists", rather than "specialists". Evidently these will be most capable, their achievements can be much greater, at personal level, at team-work, at country level, and at world-wide level.

3-. Parents must put everything on their part, so that children, as rapidly as possible, become interested in science. I am not speaking of *forcing them* in any form, so that they like science, which would be counterproductive. I am talking about giving them the opportunity to be in contact with the different branches of science, so they can decide if they take that route or not. I am solely speaking of not denying this opportunity to them. It helps this objective if we provide them with educative toys (i.e. not expensive microscopes) of several types, and playing with them, but obviously that is not remotely sufficient. Scientific books, in accord with their age should be also provided, as well as watching scientific TV programs, in order to help them to direct their interests into this fabulous adventure.

4-. In previous paragraphs it was mentioned the "comfort" the consumer has in general with respect to science. Why should the public in general be interested seriously in science?

   a. For general culture. The advance of science is so quick, that we are required to look for, to find, and to learn, from the daily advances that are made.

   b. By personal and familiar convenience. The mentioned advances can be very important, for example: −to save our life by some recent medical innovation−, or to alert us of dangers of many types, for example: the danger of skin cancer, due to solar exposure, etc.

c. Science, or rather the scientific method, allows us to detect the countless falsifications, and existing lies in all the scope of our society. The use of the scientific method has been, and is the key for the human progress, and our hope of survival.

The scientific method is based on two premises: *everything* must be questioned (*skepticism* in science: authorities do not exist, at most experts) and *experimentation* in order to be able to evaluate results (evidence), that solely indicate an approximation to a degree of certainty that could be obtained. In science there is not *absolute* certainty about anything.

Why there exist so many people who have blind faith in some "fact", because they read in some book or magazine, or because they saw it in TV"? That is because they have not found out that the scientific method exists. In relation to the product announcements (marketing), I believe that if the scientific method were used, it would be much more difficult to fool people. As a result, the industry in general, would be forced to be responsible with their products. With respect to marketing, if the consumers demanded respect, and they did not allow that their intelligence becomes insulted, the "creatives" would have to change their advertising tactics. Ads would have to become based on truth, and thus promote credible (logic) campaigns, that show education and respect.

This would require a true "creative" to make this type of work. It is very easy, using vulgar and erotic material to make successful campaigns today because we have allowed it. It requires much intelligence, good taste, and education, to make a successful campaign, without using these current cheap techniques.

Pseudoscience, like astrology, and other activities, such as reading of hands or coffee, etc., which are evidently false, since they do not produce the foretold results, only exist because the people have not taken the time to read scientific books.

I remember an old movie, that had something to do with a very popular guy (Andy Griffith?). In this picture, this individual, that had a very numerous audience, at the end of one of his programs, the responsible to switch off the mike, by mistake leaves it on, while the audience can see the actor saying good bye waving his hands. Nevertheless, what he says, and the public listens to, does not correspond to such happy waving. He says something like: "stupid pigs, how dumb you are, etc." It is assumed that right there comes to an end the popularity of this guy.

Why is this story mentioned here? That is how exactly, I imagine most of the "creative" of the large advertising companies. Perhaps, mostly when ads began to become so vulgar and stupid. Maybe the manager of the "creative", or a colleague could have said: "Hey, don`t you think that this ad is too vulgar?", or "don`t you think that this ad is "insulting the intelligence" of the readers of this ad?", and his answer, I imagine it very similar to the earlier one, i.e., do not worry, it will be directed to "stupid pigs, dumb, morons, etc." Because if it is not the case, I do not understand their lack of respect and logic. Why has marketing (and many others areas), arrived to this level? Literally because us consumers, voters, contributors, etc., thus so allow it.

The following article is extremely illustrative, taken from: *Visions of technology*, written by Richard Rhodes, illustrates the fantastic change that has happened; the beginning of the radio era began with some election, and it was being tested as an effective way to advertise politicians, and also, would promote global communities, and that would eliminate demagoguery. In addition, mass education, and culture, finally could be promoted, that could show the greed of governments and corporations. All religions were very happy, due to a new way to fast and effectively catechesis the masses.

At first, the broadcasting owner was excessively preoccupied with advertising, because he was afraid that some of his listeners, not accustomed to that annoying noise, would get angry, and change to another frequency.

Of all those desires, what was accomplished? Not a bit, but rather the contrary. The broadcasters, at first, being very careful about disturbing the listeners with ads, today, it has become a maddening torment to hear the amount, length and repetition of "pauses" in every radio or TV station, every few minutes. I, as a rule, do not listen to radio or TV at all. I just can't stand it.

¡What interesting point of view of the owner of this radio station, during the beginning of the radio era! ¡What respect, or at least what fear existed with relation to his audience, and to their possible discord, annoyance and possible boycott! ¡How things have changed! Even more truthful, how *we have allowed* them to change. Since long ago, that small respect for the radio (and viewer) audience, does not longer exists. It is evident, that the lack of respect for the audience, will continue to get worse, without limits.

What about the lack of respect of the politicians, supposedly our servants? Unless, each one of us, or at least a great majority, we energetically are against, by means of a strict boycott to this, and all the others grievances that we have let ourselves to be imposed upon.

Complexity

Given that science mostly studies experimental facts, these are, in countless forms in nature, and are necessarily complex in the extreme, if they weren't, probably we could be able to known them completely. Therefore; I will comment below, the beauty and importance of complexity.

I have the luck, that I happen to like complex things. It is not that I go through life, looking for complex existing things. Rather, when I encounter such complex things, they attract me immediately, they provoke me the "capacity of astonishment"; Engineering, Mathematics, Jai Alai, Jazz (and Classical) music, Science in general, and within it, especially Cosmology and Biology (Evolution). These activities help develop intelligence and provide much intellectual satisfaction.

In the macroscopic order, the universe is a beauty, its dimension and complexity, leaves us amazed. On Earth, nature is full of beauty, diversity and complexity, surprise us. In fact, I think that this taste for complex matters should be much more widespread in most people, if not innate. We ourselves are highly complex, our body is made up of trillions of cells.

At micro-level, a "simple" cell is amazingly complex. All factories in the world cannot perform, even remotely the quantity, complexity and in the required automatic sequence, all chemical reactions necessary to maintain life, let alone its own reproduction.

Such biological complexity is based on information, or in other words, information that is processed according to a recipe, encoded in the DNA (deoxyribonucleic acid) in the genes. As well as a computer requires hardware (a machine) and software (a program) to work properly, so the cell requires software (DNA) and hardware consisting of nucleic acids and proteins.

Our brain consist of about 30 billion neurons. Each of these is connected to other 10 thousand and many of them have 50 thousand connections. Why on earth, such complexity developed? To be content with all such monotonous, primitive and vulgar activities that invade every glimmer of our modern lives?

In contrast, I am astonished to see, on a daily basis, most of the people (very few exceptions) that are attracted, or at least passively accept, the amusement of; books, sports, "music", etc., of a sickening monotony, reflecting an absolute lack of creativity and imagination.

In the book *1,2,3 Infinity* by George Gamow; a truly infinite, as it is the "number of all numbers", or the "number of geometric points on a line". Can we say something else on these numbers except that they are infinite, or two different infinities can be compared to determine which of them is "bigger"? Does it makes sense to ask; "is the number of all numbers greater than, or less than the number of points on a line"? These questions, considered to be at first sight, without sense, were resolved by the notable mathematician Georg Cantor, who can be regarded as the founder of the "arithmetic of infinity". Speaking of greater or lesser infinites, we have the problem of comparing numbers that we cannot mention, or write, but ingeniously we can compare two infinities. If we pair two groups of both infinite objects, so that each object in the collection of an infinite, forms a pair with an object from the collection of the other infinity, and no object for both infinities is unpaired, both infinities are equal. However, if such distribution is impossible, and in any of the collections there are objects without a partner, this collection of objects in this infinity is larger than the collection of objects, from the other infinity. This way of determining infinite appears to be the most reasonable, indeed, it is the only way to do so, but beware, we must be prepared to meet with interesting surprises when applying this logic. Take, for example, the myriad of even numbers and the myriad of odd numbers. You presuppose, of course, that there are the same amount of even numbers and of odd numbers, and this agrees in full, with the above-mentioned rule, because you can establish a correspondence one to one as follows:

1 3 5 7 9 11 etc.
2 4 6 8 10 12 etc.

There is, in this table, a number that corresponds to each odd number and vice versa, so the infinity of even numbers is equal to the infinity of odd numbers. ¡It is truly simple and natural! Now, what infinity do you believe is greater; the amount of all even and odd numbers, or the amount of even numbers only? Of course, you will say that the amount of all numbers will be greater, because it contains all even numbers, and additionally all odd numbers. But this is only your impression and in order to determine the correct answer, we must apply the rule mentioned earlier to compare two infinities. And when using it, you will notice that your impression was wrong, as you can see below:

1 2 3 4 5 6 etc.
2 4 6 8 10 12 etc.

According to the rule to compare infinite sets, we are forced to conclude that the infinity of even numbers is exactly equal to the infinity of all numbers. This seems paradoxical, given that even numbers are only a part of the set of all numbers, but we must remember that when we operate with infinite numbers, we find different properties. In fact in the world of the infinite, *a part may be equal to the whole.*

Following the rule of Cantor to compare infinites, you can prove that all fractions such as 3/7 or 825/9 are exactly the same as the total of all integers. All regular fractions using the following rule can be placed. First write fractions whose sum of the numerator and the denominator is equal to 2, there is one such fraction 1/1. Next, write fractions whose sum is equal to 3: these are: 2/1 and 1/2. Now those whose sum is 4: these are: 3/1, 2/2 and 1/3 and so on. Following this procedure, there will be an infinite sequence of fractions containing all the fractions, that you can think. Now write above of this sequence, the sequence of integers and you will see that there is a one-to-one correspondence between the infinity of fractions and the infinite number of integers. Therefore they are exactly the same.

So what?, you can say, but that does not mean that all infinities are equal among themselves? Are they? And if that is the case, why compare them? It turns out that, no, this is not the case, and a greater infinity, than the number of integers and fractions, can be easily found. It can be shown; that the number of points in a straight line, is greater than the number of integers and fractions. It can be shown; that the number of points, within a line of 1 cm., 1 meter or a kilometer in length are exactly the same. It can be shown; that the number of points in a line, a square, and a cube, are exactly the same. Finally; it can be shown, that the number of geometric curves is the largest numeric infinity known so far. By which the sequence of numbers, including the infinities can be written as;

1, 2, 3, 4, 5, 6.... $\aleph$1, $\aleph$2, $\aleph$3.............. where $\aleph$0, would represent the number of all integers and fractions, $\aleph$1 represents the number of all geometric points, and $\aleph$2 represents the number of all curves, while no one has been able to find a collection of objects that can be described as $\aleph$3. "$\aleph$" (Aleph) is the first letter of the Hebrew alphabet. I ask myself? Could it be possible that the Mandelbrot set, that is, the mathematics of fractals, determined by the simple equation $z = z^2 + c$, corresponds finally to $\aleph$3? According to a video produced by the writer and producer of the picture *2001 Space Odyssey*, Arthur C. Clark, he explicitly says that such set is really infinite, which I accept as such. These short examples of science reveal, how interesting and unexpected science is.

EVOLUTION

It follows a résumé from some parts of the book: *Shadows of our Forgotten Ancestors*, written by Carl Sagan and Ann Druyan:

Homo sapiens −our species− differs from the active genetic structure (DNA) of a chimpanzee, ours closest relative within the animal kingdom, for as little as 0.4%. Only four tenths, not even ½ %, extremely scarce margin, is it not? Also, the chimpanzee is the closest relative to man than to any other species of ape.

¡How problematic has been to accept the theory of evolution of Charles Darwin, is totally understandable! We would have preferred, that ours nearest relatives had been the angels, unfortunately that was not the case. Hardly can be expected to read a book about chimpanzees, which does not include an important reference, to the famous English naturalist, activist and primatologist: Jane Goodall, who has dedicated all her life, to the study of our ignored close cousins in Africa. In Africa she met paleontologist Louis Leaky, who invited her to participate in the excavations of hominids in Orduvai, and later, to lead a project study of wild chimpanzees in Gombe, Tanzania.

Africa changed her life forever. After observing the behavior of wild chimpanzees for months, one day she discovers an individual introducing a stick (which previously had been cut and the leaves removed) into a hole of a termite mount, to get termites to eat them. With this discovery, she showed the false concept that until then prevailed: that the human species was the only one that could manufacture and use tools. Her comments on their instrumental behavior, hunting habits, social structure, their emotions, their intelligence, and their individual personality, revolutionized biology and our perception on chimpanzees and Homo sapiens. She was a pioneer in the research of great apes in the wild, by introducing original methodologies, which were criticized by the scientific establishment of the time, but which are today widely used. His research continued for decades, and even now, fifty years later in Gombe, in what constitutes the longest research on a species. Her career has been widely recognized and distinguished with many awards. Today, she spends less time in Africa and 300 days a year giving lectures and talks all over the world. Her observations and discoveries about chimpanzees, the closest evolutionary genetically to humans and bonobos, have had a huge global impact and she has become the best-known scientific women of the 20th century.

Lacking university training to conduct her research, Goodall noted things that strict scientific doctrines could have overlooked. Instead of distinguishing chimps by numbers, she gave names to each, which had their own personality, who were capable of rational thought, and feel emotions such as; joy and sadness. She noted that behaviors involving love, kisses, hugging, and even tickling they performed, believed to be exclusive of humans. These activities suggest similarities between humans and chimpanzees, that not only depend on the genes, but also concerning emotions, intelligence and family and social relations.

Goodall research debunked two beliefs of those days: that only humans made tools, and that chimpanzees were only vegetarian. Louis Leakey commented on the discoveries of Goodall; "we must redefine man and the tools, or accept chimpanzees as humans". In contrast to these nice and lovely attitudes, she also noted the aggressive side of the chimpanzees, as for example, they systematically hunted small monkeys. Goodall mentions that; "during the first ten years of study I thought... Gombe chimpanzees were, mostly, much better behaved than humans beings". Suddenly, they could be brutal, as they, like us, have a dark side. These findings revolutionized contemporary knowledge of their behavior, and resulted in evidence of a more complete social similarities between humans and chimpanzees, although in its more obscure form. Leakey obtained funds to send Goodall at Cambridge, who had no title, to study a Ph. D. in Etiology, being the eighth person to achieve this feat. Jane Goodall is very much excited to work with young people, and despite her comment; "It is very easy to feel overwhelmed feelings of hopelessness, when we see the world...", she is optimistic and has hope due to; the human brain, the indomitable human spirit and the determination of young people. And she concludes by saying; "Live in this new millennium with hope, because without it, everything you can do is eat and drink our last reserves, and observe the slow death of our planet. We have faith in ourselves, our intellect, our indomitable spirit and our young people. And we must do the work, that must be done, with love and compassion."

Because it happens that; "we have been struck hard" time and time again. Consider the first great deception that happened when we found out that the theory of Ptolemy was mistaken. No, the sun did not turn around the Earth, but the other way around. This implied that the Earth was not the center of the universe, as it was believed. Later it was verified, that no, the Solar System, and not even the Milky Way, was the center of the universe, because it happens that the universe does not seem to have a center. *Serious cosmological concept error* (religious biased, of course). Also, the thought that the earth had existed only for around six thousand years. The actual estimate of time for the existence of the Earth, is of approximately six billion years. *Serious geological concept error* (religious biased, of course). In some religions, it is believed that God *directly* created man, at his image and similarity. *Serious evolutionary concept error* (religious biased, of course).

Then, before the scientific evidence, we do not have other reasonable choice, but to accept reality. And the sooner that we accept it, as openly possible, the better chance that we have, to improve personally and as species. And in order to know us best, we ought to know very well, our nearest relatives, the chimpanzees.

However, our species Homo sapiens has been existing on earth for 100.000 to 200.000 years. This antiquity, from the cosmological point of view is irrelevant, but from the point of view of the generations that have lived, is relatively considerable.

Without feeling sorrow for ourselves by accepting the demonstrated theory of evolution, and accepting totally our reality, I think that it is feasible, and necessary and extremely desirable, that the approach of our species Homo sapiens, can and must be transformed, as soon possible, *conceptually*, in another species "Sapiens homo", in other words, intelligence truly guiding and controlling the animal, not the other way around, like until now

The difference? Humans, without denying our "animality", resident in the primitive part of the brain called complex-r (R of reptile) should "transfer" its influence to our cortex, as soon as possible, by means of the "the improvement of our intelligence", so that we abandon our neglect to the wise utilization of our magnificent potential intelligence, as until now we have done. We do not have much time left. Our survival depends upon this change. Also, in which other way can be conceived civilizations type I, II and III?

All computers are improved by the computer proper (hardware) and/or the operating systems i.e.; Windows, and other programs i.e.: Word and Exel. Given that humans already have a marvelous brain (hardly, to be improved, at least in the short term), what we can do and should do, is to upgrade our operating system (our software). And which is the unique and evident way to improve it? Well, by means of the; *Perfecting of our Intelligence*, in an integral manner, considering human education with wisdom, which I present next.

WISDOM

I have proposed in this book the necessity of the improvement of intelligence. But one thing is intelligence, and a very different thing is the use of that given intelligence. Therefore, the question is: how is it recommended to use well our intelligence? To use our intelligence well; is to live a healthful and balanced life, which can be detailed as follows; (extract taken from the essay: *The Wisdom* from Dr. Robert J. Stemberg, Yale University):

He suggests; to develop creativity, in other words: invent, or innovate and be moral.

The great equation that we obtain when combining the following elements is this:

Knowledge + Intelligence + Creativity + Morality = WISDOM

The wise person determines the right priority, and then solves the problems well. He knows that the only thing sure, is the change of everything, and that learning is a never ending process, and he tries to be fair, to the desires and needs of other people. A wise person, is that person that changed the world by its mere existence thru his/her life.

As we can see easily, there is a lot of room to advance, supposing we take all the possible measures, not to destroy ourselves, in the near future.

Given our very fast technological advance, it may still be feasible to avoid disaster, if and only if:

a.   Drastic actions are taken immediately at global level to protect us of all the dangers mentioned (as well as the ones not mentioned) in Chapter Two (and others dangers that may appear).

b.   The powerful nations really help emergent nations, so that everybody obtains a reasonable life quality.

c.   The powerful nations stop all military actions and invasions.

d.   In some way, acceptable moral values return to the restoration of the family, base of our civilization.

e.   The educative level is of excellence, and at global level, being the education of science, and the improvement of intelligence, the fundamental tools.

Impossible? If, not considered and tried with great tenacity and urgency, it will be. Due to our actual situation and its very strong inertia, it can be regarded as *almost* impossible, but feasible. If, I had considered this cause totally lost, I would not have bothered in writing this book.

But, it will be feasible only if millions of people, everywhere in the world, are convinced that it is possible, and decide to support, to boycott or to demand accordingly upon each case, all measures that are advisable, or necessary, to arrive safely, at least to the XXII century.

Could it be possible that ants and bees, are much more intelligent than the deluxe chimp, when it comes to survival? Could it be possible that the deluxe chimp, greed and avarice, are stronger than his conservation instinct?

I trust that our present behavior is reversible. Our only hope is that true national leaders arrive, and become elected. That they carry great vision, intelligence and wisdom, that feel themselves as world citizens, rather than "patriots", for their country of origin. The time of "patriotism" must come to an end. All the actual acute problems are worldwide problems that must be tried to be solved accordingly.

We must think and act having in mind our children, grandchildren and future generations, by not robbing their natural resources from them. I think that perhaps, the severity of the combination of the problems mentioned in this book, *could force*, all nations to unite as the only alternative of survival.

All the necessary changes, required to revert the actual world situation, imply a radical attitude change, in most of the deluxe chimps worldwide, which only would be possible, if a dramatic change in values, could take place. Such change, must necessarily include, the adoption of the long ago lost values.

DIAGRAM OF PRESENT CIVILIZATION
BASED ON HOMO *SAPIENS*

Present situation: Burden and fast tendency

to barbarism (towards Level of

Civilization - 1)

Globalized Planet earth is egoistic and unjust where it prevails:

Lies, exaggeration and use of low human

instincts in marketing campaigns

To have, by any means, is the only important thing in life

"Limits to Growth" recommendations disregarded

Stupid, degrading and vulgar entertainment

Avarice without limits of nations/industries

Drug invasion in all criminal forms

Mistaken use of science

Overpopulation

Peak oil

Climate change

Etc.

INPUT

⇩

BRAINS (Hardware)

Garbage in ⇨   Process   ⇨ Garbage out

OUTPUT

⇩

Less and Less   =   Raw stupidity & tendency

Global intelligence   to self destruction

UNSTABLE CONE THAT IT IS ABOUT TO COLLAPSE

Explanation of the diagram based on Homo sapiens performance: we now have the globalized planet earth, in an egoistic and unjust form, extremely equivalent to a feudal world-wide government. The harmful and perverse behavior described in Chapter Two and where they appear as INPUT, some of the present urgent problems (Predicaments). Although, the majority of the people, is not conscious of these problems, contained in the INPUT, without doubt, some of them, are causing some types of damage in their brains, that at least, cause tension, desperation, and frustration. Many other problems cause mental damage directly. In sum, this kind of problems, does not encourage the intelligent thought, but all the opposite, and by that reason, I mention them as "garbage". A computation axiom says; "garbage in (INPUT), garbage out (OUTPUT)".

I do not believe that, it is difficult to understand, that if our civilization has managed to prosper, and when so doing, multitude of serious problems have been created, that seem insoluble, if continuously and dramatically, the global intelligence is being reduced, the present base of our civilization, —the base of the cone in the diagram—, rather sooner than later, will become unstable, and therefore will tip over.

THREE

Knowledge and generalized application of science

"The culture of the mind is nourishment for the human mind"
Marco Tulio Cicerón

The pleasure to destroy

As president Reagan, had as his advisor: Edward Teller (THE REAL DR. STRANGELOVE EDWARD TELLER), (THE BATLLE FOR THE H BOMB), without a doubt, the most dangerous scientist ever to have existed, since not only was a scientist, in addition he was a politician, who managed to convince at presidency level. Along with Stanislaw Ulam, Teller designed the first hydrogen bomb. Teller also was influential, in the decision by the Truman administration, to produce the bomb, over the objections of the scientific community. His testimony, against physicist Oppenheimer, made Teller a pariah to many of his colleges, further diverting his career, to defense politics and causing him profound sorrow. Some old associates refused to speak to Teller for more than 30 years. The model for the title character of Stanley Kubrick; –Dr. Strangelove–, Teller became the leading proponent of major weapons systems like, Star Wars. He arguably became the most influential scientist of the Reagan Administration. He was very proud of a second lab, and a second weapons system –the hydrogen bomb-. Livermore is still the place where new weapons, will continue to come from.

The pleasure of finding things out

It follows a résumé of material from the book: "Our Forgotten Ancestors" written by Carl Sagan and Ann Druyan: Richard P. Feynman was a notable scientist. He said that he was physicist not for the glory and the prizes, but because he was very amused, by the mere pleasure to find how the world works, what makes it beat. So it was, that, when one early morning he was waked up, by a journalist to tell him that the physics Nobel prize, had been granted to him, Feynman answered to him annoyed: "and could you not wait until morning to tell me?".

What it really interested him was the pleasure to discover how things work. That the results of his work were useful for other scientists. The honors bothered him deeply. When they named him a member of the National Academy of Sciences, he resigned, as soon as he discovered, that what interested that organization was not to promote and to comment on scientific discoveries, but to discuss only whom to admit in this organization and to whom not.

His father was a uniform factory sales manager and he teached him, as a boy, that a person dressed in a uniform, continues to be the same person, when he is without the uniform. The venerated personages, that have uniforms or titles, often are venerated not because what they have obtained, but by the mere fact of his trophy.

Like all good scientists, he worried to spread science at all levels. He was a very beloved and solicited professor for post-degree level. Very frequently offered talks on science to the general public. He constantly warned about the deceits of all the pseudo sciences, the marketing campaigns, and mainly, of the image form as it is promoted by the political candidates (without some serious proposals), in almost all the nations of the world.

When his thesis director requested him that he presented his project before scientists of great reputation, he remained paralyzed of fear, but like in that, and other occasions, that he had to present or discuss with scientific peers, as soon as he initiated his presentation, he would forget with whom he was dealing. He would argue with awarded Nobel prizes, saying to them; "you are wrong, it does not work that way, you are crazy".

When invited to integrate himself to the atomic bomb development project, the rejection to the invitation was his first immediate reaction, since this would prevent him from continuing dedicating himself to finish his doctorate thesis, that constituted an extremely important goal of his life. Half an hour later, he had reconsidered that it was his duty to accept, since Germany was working on this same project. He was the only person present at the first nuclear detonation, without protective eyeglasses, to that extent, he was obsessed by investigation.

He possessed an extraordinary sense of humor; he had a great time performing "pranks" to the military in charge of the security, and their scientific colleagues at "Los Alamos", site of the development of the first atomic bomb. With the purpose of not sharing room with other person, he placed pajamas and slippers belonging to his wife, in the other available bed (making seem that somebody had slept in), being his room (and all that building for exclusive use of male scientists). He did profit with that tactic, because even though that this bed was not occupied by anybody, nobody got to sleep there. He was amused by opening drawers and cabinets, with all sorts of locks, including combination locks.

Given that existed censorship, almost every day, he was called to request him, that his letters and his wife's letters, did not violate these rules. He continuously managed to violate with ingenuity, these rules. With talent, he always invented new forms of communicating; "key phrases", a point at the end of his signature, would meant something, that had been accorded previously. He tried to receive encrypted messages, the key was asked to him by the censors, but he did not know the key, because Feynman requested that encrypted messages were sent to him —without its key—, so that he would entertain himself, discovering the key. He mentions and recognizes as absurd, illogical, and cruel, the celebrating of all scientists by the "success" of the explosion on Hiroshima, at the same moment in which thousands of people were already dead or dying in Japan. He blamed himself, for not deciding to work any longer in that project, when the initial reason; to have the bomb, before Germany could produce it, no longer existed, since Germany had surrendered. For a long time, he felt great depression and repentance.

Surely, you will have within reach; your computer, Laptop, your cellular telephone or Ipod. Please, estimate the weight of each apparatus. If you have never been astonished with respect to the modern wonders, this can be the moment. Dedicate a moment to try to understand, the complexity of these "art works of technology and modern engineering", that almost have not weigh, almost do not occupy volume and they cost, not very much. So that you can have a comparison parameter, let us be reminded that the first world computer, the ENIAC (Electronic Numerical Integrator And Calculator) patented in 1947, measured 100 meters in length, was formed by 30 enormous cabinets that weighed 30 tons, required enormous amounts of air conditioning, to cool its almost 19.000 tubes, consumed 200 Kilowatts of power, it was programmed connecting great amounts of cables and switches and its computation speed was 2,6 milliseconds to perform a multiplication of two multiplicands of ten digits each one (the speed of the modern computers is measured in gigahertz, that is to say, millions of times faster). In other words; the weight, volume, operation conditions (cooling), energy consumption, facility of use (Word, Exel, etc.), computing speed and almost limitless storage capacity, connectability (Internet), etc., all this is possible, thanks to the miniaturization.

Richard Feynman, was the father of miniaturization on great scale, called "nanotechnology". As he said; "there is sufficient space down there", he meant literally at atomic level. He was the first one, who better visualized the enormous advantages of making things very small and when he spoke of very small, he talked about the level of manipulation of atoms (which already has been done). It is now possible to record the British Encyclopedia in the head of a pin (of course it is possible to read it, only by means of an electron microscope). On this scale, it is estimated that all the books written to date, can be recorded in an area of only a square meter. If somebody thinks that this cannot have practical use today, just remember that the "chips" that control the computers (and every day there are more devices of all types) are possible, and indeed they were possible by "recording pin heads", in fact, in little greater areas, with an enormity of complex circuits, only visible by means of electron microscopes, or their corresponding amplifications.

The space shuttle "Challenger" exploded in flight in 1986, shortly after its takeoff. The loss was of millions of dollars, but mainly, there were killed 6 professional astronauts and one school teacher. The Secretary of State headed a commission formed by politicians, military, astronauts and a scientist. Richard Feynman was the selected scientist to investigate the "accident". If this were not the case, probably the cause of this disaster never had been known. In some book I read something about; "true accidents are almost nonexistent, since always there exist negligence, forgetfulness, hurry, lack of verification, assumptions, badly understood savings, etc." I believe that this though is a real life fact. In addition, we must not forget, Murphy's Law: "if something can go wrong, it will" and its corollaries.

Feynman found that the NASA's managers had blind faith in their airships, granting them only a possibility of one in one hundred thousand that they could fail. In other words, they said that it would be possible to send a daily rocket during 300 years, just to find a single fault. But the engineers, that is to say, those that really knew the complex reality of the designs, manufacture, and operation of these devices, granted them a possibility of one in one hundred. That is to say, they could expect 3.5 faults in daily launchings during a year. What a world difference of criterion, between employees of the same organization. The reason for which the managers grant confidence that borders on fantasy to its rockets, it is so that they continue receiving government funds. They were prepared to run serious risks, also in reference, to authorize takeoffs not recommended by the engineers, so they could fulfill the calendar and launch schedule.

Feynman demonstrated, in a live press conference, the cause of the disaster, a gasket (O Ring) was broken when submerged in a frozen cup of water. It was known that these gaskets did not have the required safety margins, but they continued to use them, they should not have been utilized, at least, when a very cold climate existed. The engineers noticed the danger, and the managers did not listen to them. His report to the Commission was considered embarrassing for NASA, reason why it was not going to be included in it, nevertheless, Feynman judgment prevailed, at least sufficiently, to be included in an appendix.

FOUR

SUGGESTED METHOD: AN ATTEMPT TO IMPROVE OUR INTELLIGENCE

"It is necessary that thinkers think about thought"
Dr. Luis Alberto Machado

One of my favorite subjects learned at school, and not taught any longer, −for which I do not find the reason− is: *Greek and Latin Etymologies*. And I do not understand why, is due to the fact, that Spanish (as well as many other languages) come from exactly that source. I believe it to be an essential subject and should be mandatory to every student. Well, by searching for the word; "intelligence", I found: Intelligentia, −entre-ligare−, which means the ability to perceive relations and differences, etc. And, given that it is, or should be, a routine task for the Homo sapiens, similar to anything that can be learned, I believe that it also should be a mandatory subject, for every school attending children, and should be given the vital importance, that it demands. The manner to do it, is to encounter a method, to find quick ways to relate easily, in other words, to find a relational connection. Thus, it will be more intelligent, the one who can more rapidly correctly find relations, either existent or new.

When I was a child, I remember to be taken to a theatre (Teatro Iris?), where a performer (Dr. Memory), with apparently magical aptitude, could perform the following feat: he would ask a person from the audience to present any short name, or item that would come to his mind, to which the performer would assign question numbers, up to fifty. So the show would follow like in this example;

Dr. Memory would say; Question # 1 and would choose one person, who in turn, would say, for example; "Black Cat", after a few seconds of concentration, Dr. Memory would ask the second question, to another person that could be, for example; "Tomorrow it will probably rain", and so forth. When the fifty questions had been asked, Dr. Memory, again after a few seconds of concentration, will shock the audience, by questioning again the attendees, at random and indistinctly, either the number of the question, or the answer to any question number: for example:

– Tomorrow it will probably rain: a person from the audience
–Two: Dr. Memory
–One: another person from the audience
–Black Cat: Dr. Memory
And so on, for a large interval.

Apparently all answers were correct, since no member of the audience did protest. Would this performer had magic spells, or rather, had he devised a very useful and learning method such as a: "Relational Linkage" (named "Method of Relation" by Dr. Machado). I would bet for the second option. Anyway, the surprises did not end there. Following, a blackboard would be brought to the scenario, and Dr. Memory would ask for two persons that would read, from some of that day's newspaper two headers, like, for example: "The Dow Jones had a marvelous recovery today in the U.S.". And the other one:

"The president of El Salvador was taken to the hospital due to a severe pain". After the required seconds of concentration, he will proceed to write: simultaneously both phrases (one on top of the other) one left to right, the other right to left. That was unbelievable, I tell you. He, no doubt about it, had found a method for improving intelligence (and memory) a great deal, and also, to make money exploiting it. Wonderful combination.

It is evident (at least for me), that most governments in the planet are very interested, in having their citizens to have null criterion, thinking citizens are not controllable, and should they really start thinking, they would organize themselves and would not tolerate absurd laws, and/or injustices from their governments. There is only one documented case, of an exception to this situation. In Venezuela, during the mandate of President Luis Herrera Camping, Dr. Luis Alberto Machado was named *Secretary for the Development of Intelligence.*

The merit of Dr. Machado, to be called to hold so important position, is directly attributable, to one of the books written by him titled: *The Revolution of Intelligence.*

But, since the intelligence of a person, exist within each person in a given place, time and circumstances, what each person chooses to do with it, is something else. In other words, a very intelligent person might behave very unintelligently (at least, sometimes), and very often, it is the case. Nothing can be done in that aspect.

It is a very well-known, and accepted notion that, mathematics constitute the best *material and means, for the development of intelligence.* The rigorous demonstration of theorems (as well as, the solution of problems) demand great concentration, intelligence, and the necessary use of logic, deduction and induction that exercise the mind, like few other subjects. These other subjects, such as astronomy, physics, all branches of engineering, etc. for their theoretical and quantitative aspect, also depend on the different branches of mathematics.

"Pure" mathematics, are developed without a practical application in mind, at that moment, curiously, some time later, it can arise a new theory, that can use these concepts. For example: it can be mentioned the theory of Relativity of Einstein. He used the (curved) geometry that Riemann had developed years before, and for which it appeared, that there would not be a practical application.

Unfortunately, for most people, mathematics is not appealing. In good part probably because of their personal experience during the learning process, due to teachers, who did not manage to transmit the taste for that science.

How wonderful would it be, to find a way; namely a "Relational Linkage", for the improvement of intelligence, that could result very interesting, to a great number of thinking people.

That in addition, it could be entertaining, pleasant and amusing?

That in addition, it would provide great physical coordination ("dexterity") to its practitioners?

Also that, it could provide a Modus Vivendi, to its students?

That in addition, it could facilitate acquiring "poly-manias", – mastering of several activities—?

That in addition, it fomented taste, for the beautiful arts?

That this activity, in addition, helped to form and/or to improve the tenacity of its students?

That in addition, it could develop an intense passion, so that this activity was carried out, with great enthusiasm?

That in addition, it would promote "team work", to its maximum expression?

That in addition, it promoted the healthy competition, between the members of this team work group?

That in addition, it would improve the intelligence, and personal imagination, to obtain original creations constantly?

That this perfected intelligence, would enable them to understand other additional complex areas more easily, like for example, science subjects?

In other words: ¡facilitate them, to become polymaths!

I believe to have found a very effective: "Relational Linkage" with all those characteristics. This "Relational Linkage", is not my invention, it has been around, worldwide, during many years. To my knowledge, nobody has given, not even remotely, the value that I think to have found in it. What's more, it is sadly in a period of extinction, for which it is urgent to "exhume" it, by this, and other several very important reasons.

How can I affirm and "demonstrate" that it is a very effective "Relational Linkage" ? Well, by an indirect approach, by analogy, by comparing it, as objectively, as it is possible, with a form of measurement intelligence, accepted at world-wide level: the entrance examinations for companies and universities, and in particular, the GMAT examination (Graduate Management Admission Test). Like practically all intelligence examinations (including also the I.Q. test), it consists basically of finding relations (as we have seen) every time more difficult to find, according to the examination progress.

This examination must be approved, in order for the applicant to be accepted to a master degree course, at the most important universities of the world. The minimum approving grade, varies according to different universities. This requirement, guarantees in good measurement, that the accepted student possesses a level of intelligence, that presumably will allow him to graduate, and thus, obtain his/her masters' degree, and in the immense majority of the cases, it turns out to be the case.

The "Relational Linkage", to which I have been referring, is a very complex musical genre. The most complex that exists.

¡It is no other that Jazz!

What is the basis for such proposal? I have been listening Jazz for more than 60 years. When I was 10 years old, I listened it for the first time. From that very first occasion, I was astonished. During my adolescence (and later), I played trumpet, where I put all my persistence and dedication to turn myself into a virtuoso, which I was not able to become, probably due to embouchure problems.

"Imaginative cartoon # 4". In this cartoon appears the late trumpeter Harry James, with his musicians around him, and in front of him, there are three attractive young girls. One of the girls has her mouth "as it would be" if playing a trumpet (within her lips inside of the mouthpiece (exaggerated) and the other young girl says to the third: "Look at her, she is exhilarated because James Harry kissed her."

I want to leave here, very well established, that in order to obtain results (improve intelligence), it is required the profound, and persistent study of instrument(s), with the goal in mind, to try to become a virtuoso. Playing "for fun only", I don't think that will suffice. A merely passive activity —*solely* listening Jazz— will hardly produce any miraculous increase of intelligence. That being the case, since I have listened Jazz since my childhood, I would be a genius. That very enjoyable activity will produce enormous joy and much intellectual satisfaction, but surely not an apex of improvement of intelligence. In this world of ours, the passivity in this area, like in any other, may be able to cause some small improvements of some type, but definitively, it will not improve the intelligence at all. The reason is simple, evident and already mentioned above: only the person who *practices with dedication and tenacity* some "Relational Linkage", is going to be able to obtain its benefits, and this is not an exception. In fact, virtuoso instrument playing, is one of the most difficult goals to achieve, even much more difficult, for Jazz musicians.

Many years ago, I thought: "Jazz is much more interesting and of greater artistic and intellectual value than classic music since it allows *creativity by means of the improvisation*". For many years, I maintained this thought, sometimes thinking that, it was a "heresy".

Some years ago, while I was preparing Jazz seminaries, I realized that Jazz, is based on exactly the same technical basis as classic music: European Harmony and Counterpoint. What's more, even improvisation, the *soul* of Jazz, had been already mastered by Mozart and mainly by Bach. Some years back, after having reread one of my favorite books: *The Revolution of Intelligence*, I became aware that Jazz is, at least for me, without doubt, "The Method of Relation", par excellence, one of the most complex activities invented by the human mind, which I hope to "demonstrate" in this book.

I can almost listen to multitude of objections from good part of the readers. All I request from them, is the opportunity to let me expose my complete hypothesis. Also that permit yourself to learn about this subject, you can become very surprised, and with luck, you could acquire a taste that can provide great moments of joy to you, for the rest of your life.

I believe not to be mistaken, with respect to the first objection that could provoke this hypothesis. This would be: well, it is known that good part of Jazz musicians, have had great vices and their lives have been example of great tragedies. If the Jazz virtuosos are as intelligent as this guy says, they will be asking, how is it, that they have not been sufficiently intelligent to live at least "normal" lives?

I totally agree with such question, but we must remember that:

"1-. Intelligence is the best instrument that we have to profit from our own personal accomplishment and collective development.

But, by all means, that is not everything.

One thing is the intelligence that we have, and a very different one, is the use that we do with it. Environmental and emotional factors can substantially alter the real capacity of intelligence subjected to test. It belongs to a body that lives in a determined time and space." (Luis Alberto Machado).

2-. It is sufficient to read about the majority of the biographies of the "great genius" of Jazz, to find out the miserable childhood they had. Many of them reared by poor families, without education, without loving parents, and from broken homes.

3-. As a result, they received bad examples in their homes, and many of them, did not attend some university.

4-. Even for the ones that attended some university, where education was and remains very deficient and incomplete in reference to the learning of "values", that promote to "have", instead of to "be". Due to this, people is educated to achieve "success" in the professional carrier, but very little preparation to live happy lives, because nothing was done to prepare them in "wisdom".

5-. It is very well known, that the artistic atmosphere facilitates and urges disordered behavior, that causes serious damage to its members. Having Jazz almost the totality of its bases from classical music, this kind of great music should be presented, mainly in concert halls, not almost exclusively in bars, some of them "dives".

6-. The economic remuneration received by this extremely difficult activity, has generally been, traditionally offensive, while other performers without preparation, in other areas receive absurd highly remunerations. Thus, a negative attitude can result due to the daily frustration, mainly in the economic aspect.

7-. They surely were not educated in their homes and/or schools, in order to literally create a very deep aversion to all type of drugs, to try to ensure that, no matter what, any drug is not tried even once.

With complete certainty, I do not justify the Jazz musician's ill behavior, that in my opinion, shining minds have not been able to fight against the difficulties of their daily life. But with base in these above mentioned points, *I understand* the probable causes of their behavior.

Let us consider an aspiring candidate to take a masters' course test, who is very intelligent and that obtains the highest possible grades in a GMAT examination, when successful solving all the problems that have been presented to him.

I want to state very clearly, that I do not even try to suggest that a virtuous Jazz musician, will necessarily obtain excellent grades in this examination, what's more; most probably he will fail the examination. But, right now, that is not the important point. Also, let us consider a Jazz virtuoso, that will interpret several tunes, improvising his/her respective solos (developing the melodic themes). These improvisations correspond to the "problems" that must solve said musician.

This comparison is valid, since what interests us, is to verify the one "competitor" who can *"relate better"*, that is to say, who is more intelligent, independently of the kind of problem, since both will be solving complex problems and both are limited by time. On the other hand, the aspiring masters' applicant will be solving pertinent problems to his area, as well as the musician, that will be solving pertinent problems to his area.

One of the most important sections of GMAT examination consist of; solving multiple option problems (normally with 4 or 5 answers to choose from), where: the difference between "the more correct" answer and between "the slightly less correct" is very subtle. Great concentration of the applicant is indispensable, to find the correct solution.

We know that he/she has limited time for the solution of the complete examination; time pressure, but he/she does not have pressure from an audience.

He/she has the option to allow question(s) to be solved later. Answering other questions first, for which he is surer about them.

He/she has the option to review answers and to change them if necessary.

He/she, can guess and choose an answer, if not sure of the correct answer.

In the musician part; the "development" of the solo(s) also constitutes a "problem" of multiple options, but of much greater amplitude and much greater pressure for the performer, in where the options are:

1-. In the first place, he has to adhere to the Jazz "chord change" rule, that indicates the direction in which the chord may change. Jazz solos are not (normally) constructed in a "totally arbitrary" note selection.

2-. The number of notes that can be chosen whenever a sound is emitted ("correct and incorrect"), according to the rule just above mentioned) depends on the instrument register being played, but certainly there are greater than 5 possibilities. The register of the piano consists of 8 octaves (eighty eight keys). Consider a "simple" instrument like a trumpet with only 3 pistons (valves). The possible combinations are 7 (no piston pressed, to all the possible combinations of pistons pressed, except from the pressed piston 3 (only), that normally is not used. The immense majority of people when they have listened a trumpet, will have heard and possibly they will have thought, that the register of a trumpet is of approximately one and a half octave. It is extremely difficult, but possible to obtain by means of great technique *three and one half octaves from a* trumpet (MAYNARD FERGUSON 1977 CLINIC). That is to say, it is possible to produce approximately nearly 40 different notes (40 possibilities to choose). This is obtained by combining selected valves, and by varying the pressure exerted by the cheeks to the lips. The support to provide sufficient pressure to the air column is provided by the diaphragm.

3-. Since the great majority of great solos are created by virtuosos, they are, as a rule, beautiful, melodic, harmonic and rhythmic, therefore, it is possible to conclude that they made "very good relations" that is to say, intelligent. Very frequently, the solo results to be even more beautiful and interesting than the theme of the tune.

4-. The virtuoso will have to control constantly: his style, the changes in volume, accents, rests (musical) —cadence—, breathing control in (breath instruments), harmony, counterpoint, etc.

5-. Very frequently multiple speed changes exist during the execution of a solo.

6-. Very frequently multiple time signature changes exist during the execution of a solo.

7-. The musician must constantly know where he is; "musically speaking" that is to say, he must keep himself counting measures.

8-. The performer has the pressure to appear before an audience, or in a recording room. Both situations carry great stress.

9-. The performer must take care of maintaining the so vital rhythm in Jazz (Swing).

10-. The performer must remain concentrated in spite of any noise (i.e. applause).

11-. The soloist must listen very carefully, particularly in order to be able to maintain the rhythm, often the bassist or the pianist will "suggest" chord changes to him, that he can utilize in his solo or not.

12-. Very frequently, given the high costs of a recording studio, and the reduced volume of CD's that will be sold, Jazz players need that the first take is perfect, which they obtain very frequently.

13-. Also, frequently mainly for recordings of big bands, the music is totally unknown to the musicians. These very complex charts must be read (played) by sight reading. Consequently the solos are "developed" over music never practiced (not even listened) previously.

14-. The response time available to select the following note to improvise is of fractions of a second. During the extremely fast passages, it is even much smaller.

15-. Something fundamental: being music executed in "real time", (as called in computer language), evidently it is not allowed; neither the smallest hesitation, nor mistakes. In some rare occasions, when occurring that the soloist committed an error, he "takes advantage of it", this error is repeated, or adapted imperceptible and the solo continues with only the "connoisseurs" possibly noticing.

I believe that all the previous arguments are necessary and sufficient for a "demonstration" that (at least good part of) Jazz virtuous are some of the most intelligent people of this planet. I am sure that applying the described method here, the preparation of extremely intelligent people can be obtained. It must now be evident that, in order to obtain a radical improvement, not only it is required to improve intelligence, also it is indispensable to perfect the rational form of its use. Therefore, all the educative system requires to be reviewed and modified to obtain such aim. Education at home, hopefully also could be improved, so that it becomes much more compatible with the schools and colleges, where education could be perfected by the utilization of the mentioned method. It is advisable to remember that the musical education of children must begin almost from conception, after this event, every passing day begins to be "education behind schedule".

The second alternative for "demonstrating" that the suggested "Relational Linkage", is the best procedure (to date known by me) to improve intelligence, is based in an extract of the following paper. In italic letters, I include my appropriate commentaries to each point of the program: *Components of a well developed thinking skills program* written by Dr. Arthur L. Costa:

"After experimenting during the last the ten years, we have learned that an affluent balanced program to improve intelligence, must include, at least, the following four components:

1-.   Content selected with good judgment.
2-.   Education in abilities of thought.

3-.   Provide demanding tasks that require the application and reflection on abilities of the thought, those that will tend to enhance intelligence.

4-.   To create an attitude towards certain habits of the mind.

The relation of these components, might be illustrated as follows:

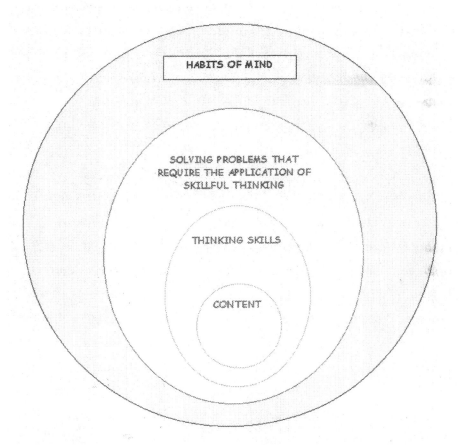

1-. The central circle represents the contents, or the subject, where the problem will be solved. The selection of a relevant matter is very important, firstly because the abilities of thought cannot be developed in vacuum. There must exist something about what to think, and also the nature of the selected discipline, imposes certain limitations, in the solution of the stated problem. The content does not constitute an end, but rather a vehicle that it activates and "it hooks" to the inquisitive mind.

The "Relational Linkage" suggested, applies very well to this proposed criterion, the deep study of Jazz, including by all means playing of instrument(s) tending and requiring virtuosity: In fact it fits perfectly and could it be considered itself like an ideal content for the improvement of intelligence. There are several reasons, mentioned in this book, that indicate that it could be extremely effective, for the improvement of intelligence. Music is a wonderful vehicle, and a relevant matter to "fire" both cerebral hemispheres, permitting great participation of the mind.

2-. The following greater circle represents learning in different abilities of thought. The investigators and the specialists agree that those constitute the basic tools of the effective thought. The successful person in school, work and life can be given, if we know and we apply certain suitably functions such as: remembering, comparing, classifying, inferring, generalizing, evaluating, experimenting and analyzing. Although these capacities are innate, their refinement, procedure and application can be improved by means of their teaching.

In order to be able to become a Jazz virtuoso, all (or at least the majority and surely other additional ones) of the above mentioned functions must be habitual and indispensable activities of the performer. Additionally, in order to be able to make "amazing and gracious" improvisations, imagination, creativity and very ample capacities for solution of problems (the development of the solos), impeccable execution, impeccable team work, tenacity, hard work, total confidence in himself, presentations before audiences, always looking for new "solutions", new instruments (for example: vibes, flugelhorn, soprano and baritone saxes, etc.), new techniques (for example. continuous breathing, recent intelligence, etc.) and very frequently being musical polymaths, that is to say: multi-instrumentalist and in addition, composers, arrangers and conductors.

3-. Execution of tasks that require abilities of thought.

The mentioned abilities of thought, are very rarely used in solitary form. These are used in an ample context in answer to demanding conditions, whose solution are not evident. In order to solve these problems, the abilities are organized in strategies that we call solution of problems, decision making, and creation of knowledge. For example, decision taking can require careful observation, to obtain data of different sources, to infer the causes, to compare and select different options and to predict the consequences.

I believe that the requirements described in point 3, apply almost perfectly to the activities that has to take into account a virtuoso during the development of his solos. Being music a "real time" activity, an activity in which errors are not allowed, well, not even a minimum hesitation. The decision making in these demanding conditions, whose solution is not evident is exercised continuously.

4-. Habits of the mind:

Even though the person may have these abilities and their operational capacities, he must be alert of taking advantage of the possibilities, should they appear. A mind habit includes:

Evaluation: Choosing the pattern of more productive intellectual behavior.

To have the inclination: To feel the tendency to use a pattern of intellectual behavior.

To be alert: To perceive opportunities properly to use productive intellectual behavior

To be Able: To have the abilities of thought and the capacity to carry out them.

To make the commitment: To reflect and constantly look for the improvement of the intellectual behavior.

What habits should the virtuous Jazz musician would have to acquire, <u>in addition</u> to the above mentioned in this area?

Confidence in himself

Ability to perform before audiences

Teamwork in great detail

Practice healthy competition

Learn and master very difficult materials

Extremely quickly important decision making

Learn and master other activities: other instruments, composition, arrangement, conducting.

Perform very difficult materials (i.e. arrangements), perfect the first time

Etc.

However, it is very significant to me, that this paper do not present a suggestion with respect to some recommended specific method. I do.

As a third and extremely important evidence that the inclusion of music indeed produces very important aid in the learning in children and young people, I present the following paper:

***Music and the mind* by Dee Dickinson** (founder and CEO of "New Horizons for Learning", international network of resident education in Seattle, Washington, E.U.)

"Music is the manifestation of the human spirit, similar to language. His greater exponents have transmitted to humanity things not possible to say in another language. If we do not want that those things remain like until nowadays, we must do the impossible to allow the greater number possible of people to understand its language". Zoltán Kodály: "I personally had experienced between the relation of music and the best academic development when I was director of the "Center of Creative activities of Seattle" several years ago. At that time we did not have on hand the investigation to explain why many children who took music and painting classes started to stand out in mathematics, and other children began to distinguish in abilities of language".

Recently an amount of reports have been published, that testify the connection between music and academic achievement. In a study on the ability of fourteen year old students of science in seventeen countries, the first three places were occupied by Hungary, Holland and Japan. All include the teaching of music, from kinder to high school. In 1960, the musical education Kodaly system was incorporated in the schools of Hungary due to the excellent results in the academic achievements of the children in the "song schools". Nowadays third grade students do not exist who cannot sing in tune and sing with loveliness. Additionally, the academic achievements of the Hungarian students, especially in mathematics and sciences, continues to be excellent. Holland initiated this program in 1968, then continuing Japan when learning of the experience of these countries.

Another report indicates the fact that the most prominent technical designers and engineers in "Silicon Valley", are almost all practicing musicians. *(I can presume, with confidence, that the majority of these are Jazz musicians).* A third report reveals that the schools that produced the more excellent academic achievements in the United States today, are investing from 20 to 30% of the time in the arts, with special emphasis in music.

Today the investigation that arises from the sciences of knowledge, provide useful information to us that explain these connections. As a result, the technology that allows us to see the human brain, while it is in the process to thinking, we can observe, for example, that when people listen a melody with a variety of tones and timbres, the right hemisphere of the brain activates. Also it "ignites" when people play music "by ear". Nevertheless, when people learn to read music, to understand the keys, annotation, and other chart details, then the left hemisphere "ignites". It is interesting to notice that the activated area is the same area that activates when one thinks about analytical or mathematical form (THE BRAIN OF THE MUSICIANS).

But why are the arts so important?

1-. They are languages that all people speak, that transcend the racial, cultural, social, educational and economic barriers, and that increase the cultural appreciation, as well as, they provide an alert attitude.

2-. They constitute a systems of symbols, as important as letters and numbers.

3-. They integrate mind, body and spirit.

4-. They provide opportunities for personal expression, taking the inner world, to the outer world of concrete reality.

5-. They offer ways of "flow states" and peak experiences.

6-. They create a connection without seams between motivation, instruction, valuation and practical application toward "deep knowledge".

7-. They make possible to experience the process from beginning to end.

8-. They develop independence and collaboration simultaneously.

9-. They provide immediate feedback and opportunity for reflection.

10-. They allow to use personal forces in significant senses to connect the understanding of difficult abstractions through these forces.

11-. They mix the process of learning and its content.

12-. They improve academic performance, improving social qualifications, attitudes, abilities, critical and creative thought.

13-. They exercise and develop high capacity abilities including analysis, synthesis, evaluation and "problem solution".

14-. They are an essential component for an evaluation program.

15-. They provide the means for the learning of every student.

16-. When playing Jazz, imagination and creativity, come into play.

The work of Dr. Paul MacLean from the Mental Health Institute provides additional knowledge to us, with respect to the musical education. Its "triple brain" suggests really that the human brain consists of three brains in one. The smallest part, near 5% of reticular formation, is the entrance for the majority of the sensations, and it is dedicated to maintain the automatic operation of the body, as breathing and cardiac pulse. Also, it is where the automatic behavior resides. The second part, the lymphatic system, constitutes 10% of the brain and it is where emotions, and some classes of memory reside, and well as glandular control. The greatest part, the cerebral cortex, near 85% of the brain, is dedicated to the process of thought of greater level. MacLean indicates that the lymphatic system is so powerful, that can literally facilitate or inhibit the learning, and the thought of greater level. It seems to be that positive emotions, such as, love, tenderness and mood, can facilitate abilities of thought of high level, whereas negative emotions, such as anger, hostility, and fear, can literally diminish the brain to their basic thoughts of survival.

The relation with musical education is evident, when we observe the students together gladly playing music, and when we collect data with respect to its academic achievements, in other areas. A study from Bloom in gifted musicians reveals that the majority had very positive learning experiences, with patient professors, who supported and loved them. A more thorough investigation in the sciences of knowledge, by Dr. Marian Diamond, Berkley neurophysiologist, offered information about the physiological brain changes, in relation to the learning experience, for improvement or deterioration. She has found that positive stimulating experiences that nourish learning, provide opportunities for interaction and answers, that can be in neuronal but abundant networks, which constitute the "hardware" of intelligence. The dynamic qualities to practice affluent music can be one of these types of experience.

I believe, that it is essential that music is teached during the academic period, in specific areas in addition to choir or orchestra. This is a way, in which we can assure sufficient participants in future classes, and a form in which we can offer opportunities for all the students, so that they develop their capacities fully. How can this be possible today, when so many professors are graduating without any musical knowledge? It is important, that everyone implicated in musical education unite, in order to convince the schools, so that they understand the necessity and importance of that knowledge. Meanwhile, much of the new technology available, can be implemented by any professor. By example, Amanda Amend, teacher of music of Grinnell College, has developed a series of videos called: *Your musical inheritance*. These tapes use techniques of accelerated learning to communicate the content, in dynamic and imaginative form. Kathy Carroll, professor of science in Washington D.C., has developed a cassette called: *Sing a science song,* produced by the Duke Ellington School of Arts. This tape is useful in itself, and can stimulate the students to create songs by themselves, to learn or to review his subject. My inevitable suggestion is; that music must be considered already as a compulsory "subject", as it is now: grammar or arithmetic. As for the details of the duration of such basic education, and the age at which it should begin to teach, I leave it to the specialists.

An inescapable complement, all children should learn some instrument, preferable, the one each child should choose. I strongly suggest that the electric guitar definitely should not be an option, given that with the diffusion, on all mass media that said instrument has 100% of the time, and where it is taken, as if it were the only instrument existing on the planet. And therefore, practically 100% of children would choose it, totally canceling my intention that children learn good music. The ideal way of assigning instruments among children should be that they themselves choose their own instrument, but should be one appropriate to form bands with all the instruments required for them. That way, each child can practice his/her instrument and have fun to hear, how they are improving their sound, little by little. Given that the "obligation" to take such subject, has no intention that children could take aversion on such wonderful art, but quite the contrary, if any child shows that does not have enough musical ability to take such courses, to assimilate them, or outright dislike, these children should be excused to take such courses. Also is for this reason, that I leave the details to specialists in teaching children.

For older students, the computer program: "Warner Audio Notes" in a CD contains; Beethoven's *String Quartet #14*, Mozart's Magic *Flute*, and Brahms' German *Requiem*. This, and other programs, allow the spectator to follow the chart, while he listens to the music, allows him to listen to each instrument independently, to study the chart, to know the composer, and much more with respect to the composition by means of photos, text, commentaries and several interpretations of music. Many forms exist to include music within the content of any matter, or for providing a rich background music, for courses for writers or literature, precise forms to learn mathematical fractions, and other concepts, to understand other cultures and accelerated forms to learn languages and other subjects. Dr. Georgi Lozanov, the Bulgarian inventor of the accelerated techniques of learning, has identified the most appropriate music to learn under his method. He has found out that Baroque and Romantic music, as background music offers the most worthy contribution for the learning of any subject. Using this method, the corporative programs and in schools, are managed to reduce the learning time to half.

Nowadays, all teachers, face a challenge due to the diversity of their students, reason why they require effective means to work with these differences. Music is a language that we all speak and understand. We are born rhythmical people, we lived 8 months depending on the heart beat rate of our mother before being born. Several additional examples (Guggenheim primary school in Chicago, Horton school in San Diego, etc.) where there exist demonstrable evidence that, music helps the learning in diverse subjects significantly.

If we want to obtain an impact argument for musical education, we do not have to present it only like a cultural value of our civilization. Not only adducing what does for the human spirit. We must use the information that we have at hand, with respect to the sciences of knowledge. We must investigate about the academic achievements of the music students, and make public and available for all those involved in the planning, and academic practices. We must make well-known the results of the musical education, in the development of improved abilities of thought of greater reach, including the analysis, synthesis, logic and creativity, improvement in concentration and ample periods of attention, improvements in memory and retention, and improvement in interpersonal abilities and abilities to work with others, in cooperative forms.

And then, we will be able to discuss the joy to learn, that arrives by means of listening and playing music. Peak experience, where people are thinking about what they are thinking and doing, are mixed and are experienced by the musicians. These states of "flow" produce learning, that provides its own reward. When all the educators recognize the value of music, as an integral and essential value and part of the curriculum, we will see more opportunities, so that all the students manage to be more successful.

The previous paper provides the third *serious indication* (theoretical and experimental test), of which the education and practice of music, during all the student life, constitutes an extremely powerful tool, that influences very positively in the learning of any subject, especially with the related ones to the sciences.

These three independent arguments are the basis; (GMAT examinations, the paper by Dr. Costa and the paper "Music and Mind"), support the "Relational Linkage", which I propose for the improvement of intelligence, like a specific mean within the musical scope for the deep gain by the mentioned aids for the best and faster learning.

The paper *Music and Mind* is an ample, illustrative, convincing, and invites to its consideration, and still more to its quick and generalized implementation. Nonetheless, I consider that it is not sufficiently specific, it refers to songs, romantic and baroque classic music, and on musical inheritance, but it does not propose a very conclusive specific "vehicle". That is to say, one could believe that *almost* any type of music could produce similar results. My proposal is; that hopefully Jazz is studied and it is implanted specifically, like the ideal and global method. I believe to have included most of the advantages that come intrinsically and the imaginative and creative attitude that very commonly the Jazz musicians present, not only when they are "producing" their music, but in addition to the creative surroundings that results *only,* from this music (due mainly to improvisation).

If, as testified in this paper; using songs and classical music achieves significant accelerated learning, in all the places where it was instituted, the described musical learning, what could be obtained with the method I specifically have proposed; —Jazz— whose "intention" is the continuous "resolution of problems", even for the same melody, always a possibly different "better" solution, whenever a musician develops his solo by means of the use of imagination, creativity and great intelligence?

However, supposing that the suggested "Relational Linkage" in this book, already was approved in some schools in some countries in the world, what would also be (at least) a compulsory requirement in order to really manage to prepare much more intelligent people globally?

1-. An exhaustive revision of all subjects from kinder garden to college, in such a form that includes "sufficient" theoretical musical education and instrument practicing (initiating with classic music).

2-. The subjects that require data memorization, that become presented as much as possible as relations, in such form that they become pleasant, interesting and from said relations are possible to remember the important data, far better that as is made in the present time. Also, that the intention is that the concepts are understood, and no longer continue with practices of only memorizing without understanding, in order to pass an examination.

3. Babies should listen Jazz in their homes frequently, if possible, before they are even born. Also they should listen classical music, popular music should be restricted to a minimum. Their ears should start becoming accustomed to listening good quality music, if this is not started early enough, later on, it would become much more difficult, or even practically impossible.

4-. Children, from the very beginning of school, should start to learn music theory, and some of the several available instruments, (piano to begin with) used in Jazz music. Obviously, the teachers will have to be able to teach in this elementary music level.

The serious study of music, should begin at the beginning of elementary school, and continue during all the stages of higher education. The music theory must include, among other disciplines; solfeggio, harmony, counterpoint, composition and arrangement. The practice of the instrument should be on a daily basis, and of "sufficient" duration. As Wynton Marsalis recommends; the advisable thing is to study the instrument several times a day, instead of a single very long period.

High school education would require having excellent theoretical teachers, and excellent Jazz musicians, who should be able to prepare students for the virtuosity level.

5. The children, from the beginning of elementary school, should have to learn, as ample as possible, range of sciences in order to direct them, towards their favorite area(s). The schools should provide a great amount of toys; "scientific apparatuses" (microscopes, telescopes, etc.), adapted for the corresponding level, so that children: "play and learn" all possible things with respect to science. Other formative subjects, should include formation of human beings with wisdom. Needless to say, that the love for nature is essential to inculcate into the young. Also children, must feel that the professors think that they are very intelligent, and thus the children will act in that sense.

6-. Children (all students) will have to feel and to be convinced, that this education that they are receiving, is an honor, that it is a privilege, and that they must take full advantage of it, and enjoy it. By all means, their parents and professors should be able (in knowledge and like pedagogues) to consummate, this vital intention.

7-. Throughout the course of the complete education, the students should continue studying deeply music theory with the intense practice of instrument (s) so that a considerable number of them manage to arrive at virtuosity. The interchange and frequent competition in festivals, between different schools, and universities, are highly rewarding and motivating, and thus, recommended.

Sports are also essential to develop a healthy mind in a healthy body, during all the school period.

8-. When using this method, during the adolescence, the students already will have:
   a. An enviable physical coordination.
   b. Certain degree of reached virtuosity.
   c. Fast intelligence developed by means of intense musical creation.
   d. Additional intellectual development due to the study of diverse sciences.

9-. Therefore, the students are already on their way to become "generalists". Great affinity is a common thought between scientists and artists, the described method will demonstrate, that serves to allow the formation of musician-scientists, that is polymath in the two human branches, based on the search of greater intelligence and sensitivity.

Let us consider Leonardo Da Vinci again, this remarkable artist, scientist, inventor, etc. who is considered the possessor of all the excellent and innovating knowledge, in all the activities of his time, it is a unique case.

I am convinced that the deep, systematic and enthusiastic application of the described method, can help to the formation of people who approach, at least a bit, the capacity that had this legendary personage.

In the following chapter, I will present a complementary and detailed description of the proposed "Relational Linkage".

FIVE

The "Relational Linkage" detailed

"The Intellect, is a vital and inseparable
part of the art of improvisation"
Gunther Schuller

"In this day of musical primitives, it is a breath of fresh air,
and a ray of hope, to see the success of Michel Legrand. He
is totally accomplished, educated, thorough musician, whose
writing is always sophisticated, unexpected and witty…".
André Previn

This chapter contains names of samples of "Standards" (tunes), encountered in YOUTUBE, to be established as guides, when utilizing said "Relational Linkage".

"The improvisation art has been in existence for two centuries. Bach and Mozart were two of the greatest improvisators of their time. Bach, playing the organ, would take one existing or invented melody and would explore its limitless possibilities, changing harmonies, sounds and moods. I am sure that once they could become acquainted and learn to "Swing", they could "seat" with the Shelly Manne quartet and enjoy without limit". Henri Tamianka (Founding/Conductor of the Symphonic Camerata of California) as appears in an LP record cover.

At my parents' home, I always listened classic music during our meals. When somebody is lucky to listen classic music since childhood, with all probability, he/she always will appreciate it, enjoy it, and probably will be able to "understand" and enjoy Jazz.

It has been verified that children that lived totally isolated from language, at most, at the beginning of their adolescence, they never would be able to learn a language. Being good music also a language, if it is not listened through childhood, explains why most people, "does not understand" this music genre, that was not listened in their childhood.

Following: a concept from Jerry Coker:

"This is why, to a great extent, sometimes the listener is presented with performances considered excellent, that cannot neither understand nor evaluate. This is because his "auditory memory bank" does not contain any reference to which he/she is listening. Perhaps, the style is not familiar, and the technique employed, is too complex for him. It is probable that if he had auditive experience that allowed him to re-unite and re-listen the aural experiences that were present in the minds of these performers, the familiarity would have allowed a patient attitude, understanding, and perhaps, acceptance, and even enjoyment."

How do I define "good" Jazz? I will use the following example to clarify such concept:

What would a consummated postal stamp collector, be interested in? Naturally only or mainly in "rare" stamps. Stamps that are really special, that have value due to their peculiarity, perfection, limited edition or inclusive because they contain some error, reason that constitute interesting items that are worth collecting. What interest would have this experimented philatelic in collecting common stamps that can be purchased by less than "two bits" in any post office?

Jazz seems to be the only significant contribution from the U.S. to world culture. In my view; Jazz really became interesting when Charlie Parker (circa 1940) and Dizzy Gillespie invented the fundamental rule of modern improvisation called: "chord change (or chord progression)" and was called Bebop. And became even better, when the *West Coast Jazz* was invented, which is in its purest form, *is a fusion of Bebop and Bach fugues"*.

Thus, the original African rhythms of this music, already incorporating European harmony, Counterpoint and Chord Change, allowed soloists to improvise under established melodic and harmonic rules. This musical movement is known, as, said before: Bebop and nowadays continues being the base of improvisation. The dictionary defines Bebop as: "fast Jazz music with complex harmonies and melodies". Dexter Gordon, the late brilliant tenor saxophonist, comments; "Bebop: a so simple word, a discipline so demanding".|

Now, within this musical genre, there exist, like as in all human experiences and products items of terrible, medium, good and excellent quality. There exist virtuosos of extraordinary quality; those are the ones that interest me to listen, and the only ones that I include when I speak of "good" Jazz.

What does it means to "develop" a solo? Imagine an architect of renown to whom you have given a sketch of an idea, about the design of your new house. Based on this sketch, the architect will work on his project. The architect will utilize the learned subjects during his college years (and all of his experience); he will apply his knowledge on design, his ability in the drawing board or in today`s tools: Autocad. Also all his/her knowledge referring to resistance of materials, calculus, aesthetics, his memory referring to several other designs that call her attention, perhaps takes some idea(s) from them, but mainly it will require all his creativity, if he is to present to you, a really attractive and original project. Based on all this, the architect will come to "develop the given sketch" to present to you, his complete design.

In similar form a Jazz musician carry out the development of a solo, using among other many things, his ample musical knowledge and his outstanding instrument technique to create his solo. It is important to note that normally, the solos are much more "interesting" and elaborated that the melody (theme).

From the books of Jerry Coker *Listening to Jazz* and *Improvising in Jazz*, I have taken the following ideas and concepts (intermingled with some of my ideas): "One of the most exiting events is attending to a Jazz concert, because it is related to a presentation of improvised music. That is the excitement that Jazz produces. The musicians will perform and discover each new sound, depending in their feelings and their mood, and with reference to the melody being played in that "now", and anybody that knows how to listen, will become surrounded by a musical aroma and his/her intellect astonished by the virtuosity of the solos. The performer sometimes may take suggestions from the rhythm section, or only his spontaneous, intimate and intellectual notes selection. Let's not forget that the creative process consists also in the discard of all the notes, that are not the best for that particular solo. Also, something very crucial, the time frame "obligued" by each tune (rhythm), "forces" the improviser to find each correct note in fractions of a second, in very rapid tempos, even much faster. Evidently the most profound and high level of intellectual and phycological state of the mind, must be present in the mind of the performer, that being the case, the inspiration is capable of beautiful melody creation."

Now if the concert is featuring a Big Band, !that is something else¡, especially if it is a band of renown, where all the musicians are top notch, and so the arranger. That is the equivalent of a Grand Prix, Formula 1, championship race.

A note of interest: "The absorption, display and use of the required theory to interpret Jazz is not, in any way, enough and sufficient to guarantee an interesting musical personality. All Jazz musicians will encounter that his playing style will be criticized by the listener. He could be able to develop a style that is lausy or highly intellectual, original or a copied style, and the tone, stout or soft, structured or incoherent, rough or delicate, easy-going or impulsive, exciting or boring, or a combination of all these possibilities, which can produce a musician with enormus virtuosity. The style of each musician is affected by his intelligence, personality, and the mastery of his instrument. Improvisation requires: Emotion, ear sense, intuition, and virtuosity, which reside in his subconscious mind, thus, the improvisation will come from his intelligence".

What to be careful to when listening Jazz:

"Sound: Pitch quality, which vary with each musician. Practically all musicians can be identified solely by their sound.

Technique: digital dexterity and other abilities

The consistent exactitude and sense of rhythm. All the great musicians are perfect in this time related concept

Tonal materials: The chords, scales, and notes that emphasize melody during improvisation.

Lyricism: The capacity to transmit feelings.

The selected vehicles and their different used types (blues, bebop, standard, etc.)

The utilization of many types of vehicles, the capacity of change without losing effectiveness.

The quality of inventiveness, creativity and originality."

The "phrasing", that I believe that it can be defined as the very personal form in which the melody is interpreted, in all of its details, especially during the development of his solo referring to:

How does he initiates each one of his solos: a simple or complex introduction, a part of the theme, a part from the completion of the solo of another soloist, etc.?

How does he ends his solo?

Does he utilizes long phrases? The long phrases are much more interesting, and of greater risk.

Does he utilizes special effects? (like "roaring" his sax) Is the amount of his effects measured or excessive?

Does he incorporates parts of other solos?

How does he uses "clichés" ? (frequently used phrases)

How does he "doubles time" ? (he plays at double speed, as the rhythm section plays)

How does he play counterpoint with another musician(s) (musical talk with other musicians?)

How does he counterpoint with himself?

How does he utilizes silences (Cadenzas)?

How does he use dissonances?

How does he use the accents?

How does he use pianissimos and fortissimos (climaxes?)

How much digitations speed does he posses?

How does he develops "fours". Interchange of mini-solos of generally 4 measures with other soloists?

Does he produce musically humoristic phrases?

Quality of his timbre (tone)?

Good taste?

Etc.

This book was to include a musical program, where I was to present a very careful selection of appropriate very interesting samples of Jazz music, burned into a CD. I believe that it was an invaluable good example, so that the reader could have an idea, of what I am talking about, when I speak of "good" Jazz. Fortunately, a publisher advised me not to do so, because of infringement of copyright materials. Thus, I selected YOUTUBE available material, in search of a second best alternative to my initial selection. Nevertheless, this alternative has a very important advantage, which is that you can watch the musicians perform, evidently not possible with a CD.

I consider the musical wealth included in this book, as one of the possible amplest samples, according to my criterion, given the tunes available within YOUTUBE, respect to the virtuosity, instrumental variety, and imagination, that can unfold virtuoso Jazz musicians. The creativity contained therein, aside from the contributed in the remarkable improvisation of a solo, reveals a deep interest and tenacity of these virtuosos, to find new instruments, new techniques, new abilities, hardly found in other areas, except, perhaps some, in classic music, several decades or centuries back.

List of selected YOUTUBE melodies:

(If the following videos, were to be omitted by some not understandable copyright rule, the objective of this book will be greatly diminished, since no standard criteria, showing virtuosos "to follow", could be a guide for the desired instrument masters of my suggested, "Relational Linkage").

The format of the description of the melodies is as follows: name of the video as it can be found in YOUTUBE (in capital letters enclosed within parenthesis), name of the melody, name of the composer and/or arranger, name of the Musician (leader of the group or big band and other members when identified), the instrument(s) played by said musician(s), and a short commentary of such tune:

(LEE RITENOUR WITH BRIAN BROMBERG STOLEN MOMENTS), "Stolen Moments" (by Oliver Nelson), Lee Ritenour, guitar, Brian Bromberg, bass, Alan Broadbent, piano, Harvey Mason, drums, Ernie Watts, tenor sax. A beautiful tune, exceptionally played.

(WILLIE MAIDEN IMPROV MUSIC CLINIC), "Four" (by Miles Davies), Willie Maiden, piano and teacher, (alto sax, baritone sax and arranger). He provided many very good arrangements for Maynard Ferguson, and latter, for Stan Kenton. In this video, he appears at a clinic playing piano and presenting his very interesting view upon "improvisation", before his students, as they improvise.

(PAUL DESMOND PLAYS "EMILY") "Emily" (by Johnny Mandel), Paul Desmond, alto sax, here we have a lyricist master, his unmistakable smooth beautiful tone and his facility for complex improvisations, like the presented here. Desmond was very gifted in language and music and enjoyed to play duets with himself ("counterpoint" with himself), as you can listen in this example.

Within a Jazz solo it is fairly common to include, a few bars of some other solo of another musician. A well performed mix, is not easy to obtain. Desmond used to mention with much humor how in several occasions, during flights, some air hostesses asked him about: "how many of you are in the quartet?"

In one occasion during the concert intermission, a well-known disc jockey commented Desmond, that he had liked very much, an inclusion of a few bars of a Chet Baker's solo. During the second part of the concert, while playing the first melody, Desmond included the portion that exactly continued from the "borrowed solo" played in the first part of said concert.

Another excellent anecdote with respect to Desmond, happened during a concert, which I had the opportunity to attend. It was evident that Paul Desmond did not feel well, for some reason. He reflected an aspect of sadness and illness, impossible to hide. Since I was accompanied by Roberto Morales, who was the promoter of practically all Jazz concerts performed in Mexico City during many years (practically all his life), when I asked him what could be the cause of that situation, I learned that Desmond had just been informed, of his father departing. Here, I was able to verify myself, the well-known saying: "the show must continue". Desmond, was remarkably affected by the bad news, was crushed, as he really felt when he was not playing, but at the moment that required his virtuous performance, he made it so impeccably as if nothing extremely sad had happened.

I consider appropriate to mention here, my friend Roberto Morales, who passed away in 2005. Roberto was the best (and only) Mexican Jazz Promoter since the beginning of the '50s. For decades, his record store was the only place where it was possible to be find "good" Jazz records. Also, during many years he was almost the only one, that would care to present great Jazz musicians in Mexico. The "Jazz/ FM" radio station, during almost 20 years presented the new great musicians.

A few years ago I attended to four recitals, where no more than 30 people in average were the complete audience. Evidently the financial result was a great monetary loss and as a consequence those were the last concerts in Mexico promoted by Roberto. Roberto`s death was an enormous loss to Jazz, since he was a great connoisseur and promoter of this beautiful music. I have certain remorse, because the last time that I speak with him he commented me that: "something terrible had happened to him". Since evidently he sounded extremely depressed, I did not want to enter into details. I assured him that I would visit him shortly. That opportunity no longer occurred, the telephone was never answered, when I wanted to tell him, that I would drop by. If another life should exist, and it is possible to organize "Jazz concerts", it is safe to say that Roberto will be in charge of such events.

(GEORGE SHEARING I`LL BE AROUND), "I`ll be around (by Alec Wilder), George Shearing, piano. The LP containing this tune, was the first Jazz music that I ever heard. That event, one of the most transcendent events of my life. Having the capacity to become astonished, I became a Jazz enthusiast instantly. Shearing, a blind English pianist who "invented" playing piano and vibes in unison, was able to keep his original group for more than ten years.

(DAVE BRUBECK - TAKE THE "A TRAIN 1966), "Take the A Train" (by Billy Strayhorn), The Dave Brubeck quartet, Dave Brubeck, piano, Paul Desmond, alto sax, Eugene Wright, bass, Joe Morello, drums. Beautiful solo by Desmond and a very interesting "fours" which is a solo interchange (usually four bars long) between two or more soloists, in this case between the piano and the drums.

(MICHEL PETRUCCIANI & TRIO – BITE), "Bite", Michel Petrucciani, piano. The virtuoso pianist Michel Petrucciani, was born in Orange, France. It is my favorite example of someone living a disastrous situation, but that has great tenacity, dignity and talent of what he can achieve. I was told, that he rests next to Chopin at the Pere Lachaise cemetery. The greatest physical problem of this great master of the piano, was centered at the lower part of his body. He was born with "imperfect osteogenesis". Nevertheless during an interview, when asked about his "problem", he replied "what problem?" Both of his legs were deformed, and extremely short, of course, he had to help himself by using very small crutches. I was lucky enough, to listen to him in person, at the "Palacio de las Bellas Artes", shortly before his death. As expected, it turned out to be an impressive and unforgettable recital. His height, hardly exceeded the bench used to sit down to play the piano. He only could sit by himself at the bench, by an almost Olympic gymnastic maneuver. The Piano pedals, utilized a special device, so that he could operate them. Fortunately, the upper part of his body (his torso), was (almost) normal, so he could not only play well, but did achieve an absolute mastery of the instrument.

Michel`s family owned a music shop, where Michel "tested" instruments for their clients, when he became nine years old. One day, a lady visited the shop, and marveled by such a wonder instrument, played by Michel, and decided to buy it for her son. Two days later, the lady was back in the store complaining, that his son could not get the same sounds, as the one she heard at that shop. Michel`s father had difficulty persuading the lady, that the problem was not in the instrument. Michel not learned to read and write, until he became nine years of age, but his father had already taught him music bases. A private teacher, taught Michel classical music later. Michel learned Jazz while still very young, because his father had heard that music, since the age of seventeen, he played guitar, and had an extensive collection of this musical genre. Michel mentions that, just as his father, he is highly selective, musically speaking. Michel, at age twelve, could copy exactly (only with his right hand he had100% the skill required for that purpose, for the left hand, that capability came later) Oscar Peterson`s solos. (Oscar Peterson was a remarkable Canadian pianist). When he became sixteen years of age, Petrucciani decided to break away from his family. Multilingual (French, English and Italian) and having studied mathematics and feeling quite well, "self-educated", he left the security of his home, to prove that he could be self-sufficient. Michel Petrucciani had a very special daily piano practice, I have not heard of any other great pianist that exercises, using this technique. This difficult and therefore extremely rare and little-known technique, is known as: "recent intelligence". The exercise consists, of playing a melody in the original note, let's say in C, using the left hand. With the right hand, playing the same melody, halftone higher, i.e. in C#. Then improvising on C#, accompanying the original note by using the left hand. It sounds really terrible, says Michel, it is wrong but interesting. This teaches him to utilize two completely independent brains, to maintain the action of his separate hands. His technique goes where his mind wants to go. Sometimes he does not have the mental ability to reach this point. That is why, he is an instrumentalist. This tool allows him to reach more than his mind.

(MARCIAL SOLAL GREEN DOLPHIN STREET), "Green Dolphin Street" (by Bronsilaw Kaper), Marcial Solal, piano, Michel Gaudry, bass, Ronnie Stephenson, drums. This extraordinary Algerian pianist, is responsible for the "Marcial Solal International Piano Competition" that take place in Paris, France every four years, where the greatest young Jazz piano players, show their best abilities.

(OSCAR & ANDRE PLAY TOGETHER), "?"; Oscar Peterson, piano, Andre Previn, piano. Peterson the "super pianist", who was; "the pianist to follow" for so many great pianists. Among his greatest amazing techniques, his ability to play both hands at unison, for very long and fast passages, is impressive. Andre Previn, is a well known conductor of classical music and a fine pianist, as well as, a Jazz pianist (once in a while), who interviews Peterson and in a grand finale, plays along with him.

(OSCAR PETERSON & MICHEL LEGRAND IN SHOW), "Look what happens ", (by Michel Legrand), Oscar Peterson, piano, Michel Legrand, piano, Niels Orsted Pedersen Bass. Another piano duo. The "le grand" Legrand piano virtuoso, composer, singer, arranger and surely, there are several additional "unknown" musical abilities.

(MARIAN PETRESCU-CARAVAN), Caravan (by Juan Tizol), Marian Petrescu (piano). Occasionally, phenomena in nature occur. An example, is the Siamese brothers, another one, the birth of a baby with two heads. Marian Petrescu is a phenomenon. As I commented to him in person, congratulating him in a concert that he offered at the "Palacio de las Bellas Artes", during 2004, I said to him: "Marian, you are from another planet" that provoked a sonorous outburst of laughter. The only form to understand his virtuosity is to consider that he has two right hands that are controlled by two connected brains. Throughout my life, in daily contact with Jazz, I have had the opportunity to listen to; "the great ones of the great ones", but Marian Petrescu, is beyond category, if you think that I am exaggerating, listen to his interpretation of "Caravan", when he was only sixteen years old. He returned to the

"Palacio de las Bellas Artes", during 2005, where I was able to listen to him in person, again. Luckily, I am a friend of the pianist Miguel Angel Rodrigo, who is a friend of Petrescu as well. Miguel Angel, with great dedication and effort has dedicated several years to arrange presentations of Marian, in Mexico. This, as well as, many other things in Mexico are far from easy. I myself, visited one of the duopoly TV stations, to try that this company could be the promoter of this event. Evidently, this was not the type of "star" in whom they are interested, nothing to do with the "top ten". After all, I proposed the promotion of art music, rather than commercial "music" of the lowest quality, which is the unique matter, that attracts the interest of this company. Some years ago, when Miguel Angel visited Europe, to take piano lessons, he met Petrescu, at that time only 16 years old. Marian commented then: "I know everything with respect to the piano applied to Jazz". This asseveration would seem pedantic, but the truth is that he indeed, at that early age, already was a consolidated virtuoso, as can easily be verified listening to his interpretation of the above mentioned melody. Indeed at that age, he obtained second place, in the world-wide competition referred also above, in this book. Petrescu declares emphatically: "I never allow myself to play Jazz without first playing Rachmaninoff". What?, he warms up, playing Rachmaninoff?

(STAN GETZ GREEN DOLPHIN STREET), "Green Dolphin Street", (by Bronislaw Kaper), Stan Getz, tenor sax. Perfection on every execution, including superb solos, was his always attained goal. The tenor saxophonist Sonny Rollings once commented about Getz; "Let`s face it, every saxophonist would love to play like Stan Getz".

(DYLAN`S DELIGHT PEPPER ADAMS), "Dylan`s Delight", Pepper Adams, baritone saxophone. So far, you have been presented 3 out of 4, members of the sax family, the other one, is the soprano sax).

(CARMEN McRAE SINGS I'M GLAD THERE IS YOU), "I'm Glad there is You" (by Paul Madeira), Carmen McRae, vocal. In this book, I talk about my appreciation regarding the scope of instruments vs. human voices, nevertheless, "there are voices and VOICES". Good Jazz singers agree fully that; "*first* they are Jazz musicians, and *later* singers". That is to say, they know and feel to sing: "phrasing like a Jazz instrument". The timbre of Carmen is "smooth, sweet and hoarse". I really consider it beautiful. For me, this is the suitable example of romantic music, where the composition is beautiful, lyrics are beautiful, the voice is beautiful and the orchestration beautiful. Is it not, what one wants to dedicate to a loved one?

(THE FOUR FRESHMEN – POINCIANA), "Poinciana", (by Nat Simon), Four Freshmen, vocal. This is my first choice regarding a vocal group. The vocal harmony they can achieve is really awesome. There has been many replacements, none of the original voices appear in this presentation, nevertheless, the timbres, the harmony, and the complete group, sounds exactly as the original quartet.

(ANDY MARTIN SOLOING ON A MINOR AFFAIR), "A Minor Affair" (by Sammy Nestico), Andy Martin, trombone. I have been following Andy since he was a teenager, in a group called: "Jazz Adoption Agency", commanded by the drummer Dick Berk. He was very good, now he is superb.

(FRANK ROSOLINO ITALY 1970`S W/CONTE CANDOLY), "Sweet and Lovely" (by Ella Fitzgerald), Frank Rosolino, trombone, Tony Scott, baritone sax. I consider him, as one of the 5 greatest trombonists of all times.

(FRANK ROSOLINO & RAUL DE SOUZA – CORCOVADO), "Corcovado" (by Antonio Carlos Jobim), Frank Rosolino, trombone, Raúl de Souza, trombone. Now a trombone duet, featuring a great

Brazilian player. Notice how well they "counterpoint". I believe that almost the only contribution that popular music has ever given to Jazz is, the "Bossa Nova" rhythm and "feeling", also some very good composers, such as; Antonio Carlos Jobim, Vinicio de Moraes, etc. But notice, for example how the piano chords are very simple and repetitive (as most "Latin" piano chords are), in comparison to piano Jazz chords.

(DEXTER GORDON - GREEN DOLPHIN STREET), (by Bronislaw Kaper) Green Dolphin Street, Dexter Gordon, tenor sax. Now you can compare this beautiful tune in three different versions.

(SHELLY MANNE QUARTET – BLUES IMPROVISATION), "Blues Improvisation", Shelly Manne, drums, Ray Brown, bass, Hampton Hawes, piano, Bob Cooper, tenor sax. Notice the smile in Ray Brown's playing, he is really thrilled.

(CLIFFORD BROWN & MAX ROACH JOY SPRING), "Joy Spring", (by Clifford Brown), Clifford Brown, trumpet, Sonny Rollins, tenor sax, Richie Powel, piano, Max Roach, drums, George Morrow, bass. Clifford Brown died in an automobile accident, not yet 26 years old, yet one of the greatest trumpet players of all times, influencing almost every trumpet player thereafter. Arturo Sandoval, the great Cuban trumpet player commented that, when he started to play trumpet, became amazed when he listened Dizzy Gillespie. Shorty after, he heard Clifford and became even more dazzled, because of Clifford`s mind bogging beautiful and very complex solos.

(LEE MORGAN I REMEMBER CLIFFORD), "I remember Clifford" (by Benny Golson), Lee Morgan, trumpet. Here Lee plays a melody composed to remember the above mentioned "genius", as Dizzy Gillespie himself referred when addressing Clifford Brown.

(FREDDY HUBBARD JOY SPRING), "Joy Spring" (by Clifford Brown), Freddy Hubbard, trumpet. A very talented trumpet player, sadly also very careless sometimes, due to his playing, at full capacity, without warming up previously, which seriously damaged his upper lip, from which he never totally recovered.

(AUTUMN LEAVES CHET BAKER – PAUL DESMOND), "Autumn leaves", (by Joseph Kosma), Chet Baker, trumpet, Paul Desmond, alto sax. Chet Baker is one of my favorite trumpet players: his lyricism (ease to transmit feelings), tenacity, loyalty to his music, his tone (timbre) and his innate musical capacity. Son of a guitar player fond of "country music", he could easily have dedicated to this musical genre. But it was not thus, for he "had Jazz music inside", the proof is that the only music course that he attended, he got an "F", which represents a remarkable exception, since most of the remarkable Jazz musicians of his time, before, or later, have characterized themselves for the study of classic music, before studying Jazz. I have as a norm, not to write with respect to the personal problems of any kind, that any musician, has had during his lifetime. All of us have personal problems, some worse than others, but they are *his (or our)* problems. Several books dedicated to these biographical facts exist, as for myself, the important things are their musical contributions, not their human behavior. Recently, it appeared in TV a Jazz series by Ken Burns. Evidently it generated much interest and expectation. From the very first chapter I noticed much emphasis in the biographical facts, specially the negatives ones of each presented personage. The presentation of the artistic quality and musical contribution of each presented musician, was limited enough. The second chapter presented a similar trend, reason why by half of the third chapter, I turned off the

TV set, not watching any other episode. I understand that this type of material, is the one that most viewers interests them most.

Unfortunately Chet (as well as many other Jazz musicians), had a great deal of personal problems and as a result, he was struck criminally in his mouth, resulting in the loss of several teeth. Nothing can be worse for a trumpet player. Several dentists commented him about forgetting playing the trumpet. During that time, I studied and worked in Los Angeles, reason why I had the luck to listen to him in person at a place where I attended regularly (Shelly Manne's Hole). That happened when he was in dental reconstruction, with some dental pieces missing, reason why he could not perform a very good session, as it would be expected, but his tenacity allowed him to recover his musical capacity, not much later. His last CD`s (The Last Concert, and The Legacy), demonstrates this, when he already was about sixty five years old. He always commented that he always played, "as if it was the last time". His timbre was unique, soft volume, using a minimum of air, "like a whisper". Speaking of air, his timbre is distinguished sometimes by; "half sound, half air", very beautiful and very distinguishing sound.

(RED RODNEY – HOW DO YOU KNOW), "How do you know", Red Rodney, trumpet, Garry Dial, piano. Another great trumpet player, also hit in the mouth (this time by a cop), who also managed to play trumpet again. He commented that; "the only music that he would ever play would be Jazz and that if he could no longer perform professionally, he would play for himself only, but that he, would never change musical genre".

(SHORTY ROGERS & HIS GIANTS INFINITE PROMENADE), "Infinite Promenade" (by Shorty Rogers), Shorty Rogers, flugelhorn, Bud Shank, alto sax, Bob Cooper, tenor sax, Bill Perkins, baritone sax,

Pete Jolly, piano, Monty Budwig, bass, Shelly Manne, drums. Shorty Rogers was the "father" of the "West Coast Jazz", a very interesting Jazz style, that started in California (circa 1950). I am almost quite sure, that Shorty was the first Jazz musician to play the flugelhorn, and to include within his bands, the French horn (John Grass). I comment this because I have old LP`s that indicate said assumption.

(WYNTON MARSALIS - MOTO PERPETUO), "Moto Perpetuo", (by Niccolo Paganini), Wynton Marsalis, trumpet. Although the melody interpreted here, does not correspond to Jazz at all, the reason to include this melody, is the following; to present the virtuoso trumpet *of a Jazz musician*, Wynton Marsalis, who *also* plays perfectly classical music. If you want to verify this asseveration, listen to this beautiful and extremely difficult melody. Question: Do you believe possible, to inhale and exhale simultaneously?

Niccolo Paganini wrote this melody for his instrument, that is to say, the violin.

The duration of this melody is exactly 4:33 minutes. After listening to this melody, please reconsider your answer, if your answer was that it is not possible. It is possible, it is known as "circular breathing", and used almost mostly by Jazz musicians. Marsalis, was not the inventor of this method, but he is the most impressive of its executants who I have listened.

(GEORGE COLLEMAN & AHMAD JAMAL MY FOOLISH HEART), "My Foolish Heart" (by Victor Young), Ahmad Jamal, piano, George Coleman, tenor sax. Another good example of "circular breathing", this time by a sax player that you can see, if you watch his cheeks closely. I consider this melody one of the most beautiful and romantic ever composed.

(CARMEN MCRAE - My foolish heart (Recorded Live at Bubba's)). A voice interpretation of the above tune. The final part includes a Jazz invention; –scat-, which is a vocal reminiscence of instrument playing).

(RON MCCROBY EL MEJOR SILBADOR DEL MUNDO), "Wave" (by Antonio Carlos Jobim), Ron McCroby, Whistling (Puccolo). It is very common, among Jazz musicians to be polymath (musically speaking). The reason: they have so much love for their music, that they diversify as much as possible. This can be accomplished by: mastering of several compatible instruments (saxes) or even very different instruments, to invent and/or to modify instruments (slide to valve trombone), to compose and/or to arrange music, to invent diverse complex techniques; (high range trumpet playing), etc.

In this particular case, Ron McCroby, played clarinet, flute and sax(es) and specialized since adolescence, in whistling. But I mean, *truly whistling*, with a purity and beauty of sound and a perfect intonation, as much so, that when the piccolo player of his school band became ill, Ron played the part of the piccolo – whistling–.

Great so far? Now it is time for the Gran Prix of music: (modern) Big Bands…

(DAVID PERRICO MY FOOLISH HEART), "My Foolish Heart" (by Victor Young), David Perrico, trumpet & flugelhorn & director. This extraordinary ballad is very well performed by a big band that includes a violin section.

(BIG BAND OF LISZT BLUE DANIEL), "Blue Daniel" (by Frank Rosolino), Big Band of Liszt, a European band playing very good, with two performing soloists trombone players (notice that one of them, is left-handed).

(WOODY HERMAN REUNION AT NEWPORT), "Reunion at Newport", Woody Herman, Clarinet & conductor.

(PORTLAND JAZZ ORCHESTRA – QUINCY JONES - STOCKHOLM SWEETENING), "Stockholm Sweetening", (by Quincy Jones), not played by Quincy`s band (see next tune). These two tunes with the same title are suggested to be played in this order, one immediately after the other.

(DOUBLE SIX OF PARIS STOCKHOLM SWEETENING) "Stockholm Sweetening", (by Quincy Jones). Mimi Perrin, the great French lyricist, got hold of several Quincy`s charts (as well as some others), and transcribed note by note (solos included) for voice arrangements (four males and two females). Interestingly, the choruses and the solos contain, not only the notes but lyrics (in French). Not only that, the timbre of the original instrument(s) is "reproduced" by each performer. Listen carefully and enjoy it. That was the time when Quincy Jones wrote so many fine Jazz charts, before becoming quite commercial, and when money became more important, than art. ¡What a pity Quincy!

(ROB MCCONNELL STREET OF DREAMS), "Street of Dreams" (by Victor Young), Ian McDougal, trombone, Guido Basso, flugelhorn, Jimmy Dale, piano. This superb Canadian band that recorded and performed for more than 25 years until the recent passing of its founder, the trombone player and great arranger Rob McConnell.

(STAN KENTON ARTISTRY IN RHYTHM), "Artistry in Rhythm", (by Stan Kenton), Stan Kenton, piano & conductor. Stan`s contribution to Jazz is unparallel, his several great bands, always with the leading musicians available, and the greatest arrangers such as:

Bill Holman, Bill Russo, Johnny Richards, Pete Rugolo, Marty Paich, Shorty Rogers, Gerry Mulligan, Lennie Niehaus, etc. In the music score "Prologue (This is an Orchestra)" Stan presents his current stars soloing each, from which results evident: why the orchestra sounds like it does.

(STAN KENTON MY OLD FLAME), "My Old Flame" (by Sam Coslow), Stan Kenton, piano & conductor. This superb arrangement by Marty Paich, identifies very clearly de "Kenton" sound. Solos are by Roy Reynolds on tenor sax and Clay Jenkins on trumpet.

(BILL HOLMAN KINGFISH), "Kingfish", (by Bill Holman), Bill Holman, conductor. This and the next chart are around sixty years old, composed and arranged for Kenton`s band. To me, at least, they sound "brand new".

(BILL HOLMAN THEME IN VARIATIONS), Bill Holman, conductor, notice that this tune does not have any soloist.

(BOB FLORENCE CARMELO`S BY THE FREEWAY THE BOB FLORENCE LIMITED EDITION), "Carmelo`s by the Freeway", (by Bob Florence), arranger, conductor. Another "top notch" composer and arranger, immediately identified by his style, who as any other excellent arranger knows, who is to play each solo, because no other musician could play every bit more adecuate.

(BOB FLORENCE A TRIBUTE TO BOB FLORENCE), "Limited Edition Express", Bob Florence Limited Edition band. Here we can see the happiness (rather than a sad feeling) when playing one of his last compositions and arrangements, the tribute to Bob. We will all miss him, but will be very happy listening to his ample musical work.

(GRP ALL STAR BIG BAND BLUE TRAIN), "Blue Train", (by John Coltrane), Nelson Rangell, alto sax, George Bohanon, trombone,

Bob Mintzer, tenor sax, Russell Ferrante, piano. Watch and listen to this very good band during a tour to Japan.

(GRP ALL STAR BIG BAND CHEROKEE), "Cherokee", (by Ray Noble), Arturo Sandoval, trumpet, Randy Brecker, trumpet, Chuck Findley, trumpet, Byron Stripling, trumpet. Now also watch the whole trumpet section playing solos. Pay close attention as each trumpet player improvises his solo. Four soloists playing flawlessly, an extremely difficult and fast improvisation. Notice, in particular, the extremely high range of Arturo`s solo. Notice also, the attention with which the whole band pays, to this extremely difficult execution.

(LA JAZZ INST. CARL SAUNDESRS INVITATION), "Invitation", (by Bronilaw Kaper), Scott Whitfield, trombone, Carl Saunders, trumpet & conductor, Brian Scanlon, alto sax. A very good solo by Scott`s trombone. It seemed to me, as the debut of Scott in this band. Notice how well impressed are several of the musicians (Doug Web (sax), and Ron Stout (trumpet), by this remarkable solo. Carl Saunders a trumpet player for whom Bob Florence commented; "when he plays his solos, my jaw drops in amazement", well, mine does too.

(MIKE VAX MY FOOLISH HEART), "My Foolish Heart", Carl Saunders, trumpet. Another solo of mind bogging nature, ¡what an incredible way to play a trumpet! Notice how Bob Florence (pianist) is about to start playing, when the introduction of Saunders has not ended, clearly not even the members of the band, know sometimes what the soloist is going to "invent". Watch the bassist smiling with joy and amazement.

(MAYNARD FERGUSON PLAYS "MAYNARD FERGUSON"), "Maynard Ferguson" (by Shorty Rogers), Maynard Ferguson, trumpet. Shorty, a trumpeter himself, comments the thrill that he felt, when writing the extremely high notes, that were part of his composition, to honor what some call: "the greatest trumpet player ever".

(MAYNARD FERGUSON GIVE IT ONE) "Give it One", Maynard Ferguson, trumpet. Here a somewhat older Maynard plays one of his standards.

(ERIC MIYASHIRO GIVE IT ONE), "Give it One", Eric Miyashiro, trumpet. In this video, Miyashiro, born in Hawaii, from Japanese parents playing homage to Maynard Ferguson plays outstandingly similar to his idol. Believe me, not an easy task.

(NEWPORT UNT One O'Clock Lab Band Live from Birdland) "Newport". Conducted by Steve Wiest. Here, a *college band* from the University of North Texas, sounds like a professional band counting with accomplished musicians. Since I have the original version by the Maynard Ferguson band, it's hard to tell the difference, except for Maynard's solo. This band is exactly what I have in mind, when I suggest that school bands should be formed, all over the world, with such quality in mind. Congratulations Mr. Steve Wiest!

Of course, there has been several others notable school bands such as: *Eleven Plus*, an English Jazz band, where, as it name implies, some musicians are barely twelve years old, and let's not forget several excellent bands from Fullerton College, where the trumpet virtuoso: James Linahon was a member of its faculty (as musician and band director).

During 1999, I had the opportunity to attend a Jazz festival, organized by the "California Institute for the Preservation of Jazz". In what degree of extinction is Jazz music, that requires the use of the word "preservation"? I was able to assert, that the attendance to these concerts, was very reduced, there in California, where only fifty years before, the very important "West Coast Jazz" modality, had been created, as a very much interesting Jazz development, that attracted, during several years, the attention and taste of a very important public segment.

I listened Jazz for the first time, when I was around 10 years old. It happened one day when my older brother arrived home with a LP record featuring the blind English pianist George Shearing. My astonishment and awe when listening to it changed my life drastically. The countless moments of happiness that this music has provided me are invaluable. I could not believe that a blind person could play any instrument. Least of all piano.

What *IT IS NOT* Jazz:

Jazz is not dance music (although in its beginnings it was danceable), frequently I see announced Jazz dance classes, where, supposedly, it is taught to dance it. I can't imagine to what they call Jazz.

Jazz is not intended to be background music, all the opposite, it is necessary to listen to it with plenty of attention, because its beauty, among other things, resides in a vast amount of details displayed.

Jazz is not a music without melody, very frequently there are several melodies being played concurrently. I have heard comments stating that "everything sounds the same", the opposite results to be the truth.

Jazz is not music that lacks base and structure, but all the opposite, as mentioned above.

It seems to be the belief, that the actual popular music that has been heard, since more than half a century ago, every moment, and in all places on earth, is a direct descendant of Jazz. In nature, children often look somehow like their parents, there appear to be some evident and/or important inherited characteristics. These characteristics are often easily detectable. But detectable or not, DNA analysis, will ensure, without doubt, if there exist, or not definitive hereditary characteristics. However, as it happens in nature, parents can happen to have the misfortune of having a mentally retarded child, with Down syndrome or worse, even with dementia, but that is another subject. Referring to Jazz, this very unhappy case, where I have assurance, that no inheritance existed. Because not a single example of the complexity, beauty, variety, virtuosity, swing, creativity and improvisation, etc., found in Jazz is encountered anywhere in popular music. When hearing this modern popular "music", it is not possible to detect any similarity, but all the opposite, it does not sound, even remotely vague, like Jazz. When listening to it, and analyzing it, component by component, it is evident that not a single "gene" was "inherited". I believe that in this chapter I have spoken sufficiently about Jazz, so that it is not left any doubt in this aspect, nevertheless, I will comment here, these wide differences.

Let us consider the instrument utilized by the music genre that it is heard everywhere, all the time. The only "contribution" regarding popular musical instruments has been the grotesque electric guitar. This instrument, consists of a solid table, *without a resonance box*, and a built-in *"distorter"*. Who, in his right mind, and with good taste, could possibly design, and even worse utilize such satanic sound? This only (luckily) "contribution", I consider it, like one of the most harmful and annoying inventions (in all aspects), that has ever been devised. This instrument is used invariably, and constitutes the complete, and only basis of this musical genre. The electric bass is a variation of this instrument, therefore with similar characteristics. Any fine (Hi-Fi, not to mention Hi-End) amplifier, has as one of its more important characteristic, the low "total harmonic distortion", which must not exceed 0.08% (which self explains it, it is clear that it is a very small percentage!). So, if you can afford a terrific (tube) amplifier (they are quite expensive), you buy it, and you listen "music", that purposely includes a great deal of built-in distortion, in its only type of instrument. I give up.

The drums, in the hands of a virtuoso and elegant Jazz musician (such as: Shelly Manne), where he really accompanies the soloist, in medium or soft volume, conceives affluent thought and good taste "blows", which are a delight to listen. The "brushes" are utilized only in Jazz, and are irreplaceable while playing tender ballads. The big band drummer is something very different (such as: Stan Levey), his drive, swing, accents and volume goes in accordance to the volume level of the band, which according to the great Stan Kenton while presenting one of his great bands in the piece "Prologue": (a real good big band should be; "wide in scope, from tender soft sounds to screaming crashing dissonances"). The pop music drummer believes to be the permanent soloist and falsely senses that the quality of their "music" is directly proportional to the volume (as old the rest of performers).

Speaking of quality (or rather, the lack of), also this popular music utilizes great amounts of extremely loud speakers, lights and stages which, for a true concert, in where music of true quality is presented, they are totally unnecessary. For a Jazz concert, a single reflector could be sufficient, the "light" that is desired "to be seen", will come from the musical execution, not from stroboscopes.

What is Jazz?

In our planet, everything presents a different quality degree from 0 to 100%. Jazz is not exception, and according to the general norm, there exist very many low quality performers (with too much frequency, music of very low quality is mistakenly labeled Jazz), much of medium quality and relatively little of excellent quality.

Before presenting several of the definitions of Jazz of my own, I want to leave very clearly again, that when I talk about Jazz anywhere in this book, I exclusively talk about that percentage that is remarkably excellent in all its aspects.

Definition of Jazz: Dave Brubeck, defines this music genre as: "improvised music, syncopated, using rubato and dissonances, which originated from African rhythms, that later incorporated Counterpoint and European harmony". Brubeck begins his definition of Jazz, correctly as I believe that it must be, that is to say, defining its "essence" – the continuous improvisation — (its soul), and defining its "heart", that is to say, its rhythm that turns out to be syncopated, that is, accentuated in the second and fourth beats. Using rubato (robbed time) in where the value of notes arbitrarily is extended or shortened. It frequently uses dissonances, that when well used, as is generally the case, presents an interesting musical change causing not expected sounds (surprises). Originated from African rhythms, that is indeed, the origin of this musical genre, at the beginning of the XX century. When this music incorporated Counterpoint and European harmony, it became a musical genre with solid bases, that permitted it to produce quality music.

Totally agreeing with this definition I have some other complementary unpublished definitions of my own:

"Jazz is: anti-monotony par excellence".

Being the improvisation, the soul of Jazz, any melody being interpreted by any musician will contain different solos, on every occasion that the melody is played. The melody theme may or may not be "respected", but all the solos will be very different.

Among the benefits of Itunes, is the easiness for selecting the order of playing the tunes. One of the most illustrative "anti-monotony" demonstration, is playing the tunes "selected by name". In such a way, that when you happen to have the same tune recorded by several artists, you can appreciate the very different solos, as well as, the very different "approaches", and arrangements displayed. For example; I happen to have the tune; *all the things you are*, played by 22 different virtuosos, in different settings, such as: a recital, duo, trios, and quartets, up to several big bands. Also a great variety of instruments exist: piano, saxophones (its 4 types), vibes, trombone, trumpet, harmonica, guitar, voices, etc. In many cases, I have the same tune played by the same musician, where the solos are always different from one another. The great drummer, Shelly Manne said humorously: "we never play de same solo *once*"

"Jazz is: Joy by means of "serious" musical diversion".

As said before, Jazz, has exactly the same theoretical basis of classic music and many other exclusive characteristics.

It is worthwhile to remember that; "to play" also means, to have joy, or to "utilize a toy" —the instrument— (MAYNARD FERGUSON

CLINIC:01 A BRIEF SERMON). Jazz musicians are literally amused, when they are recording in a studio, or playing live, not to mention the very lucky ones that can understand Jazz, "get the feel", and become marveled, by the unique awe of this creative art.

From the very illustrative interviews from "Jazz Wax", I found, and took this shortened quote: "West Coast Jazz can be said that it was started, promoted and supported by the bassist Howard Rumsey (among others of course, such as Shorty Rogers), who formed "The Lighthouse" club in Hermosa Beach, where the Bebop traditional formula become worn. Rather than to feature, two or three horns, racing furiously in tight formation, West Coast Jazz was more linear. What appealed more to the ear were the harmonies —one instrument circling or supporting the other in cool counterpoint—". In short: West Coast Jazz, is in its purest form, a fusion of Bebop and Bach fugues.

Between Jazz musicians an implicit meeting of minds exists, in which during the execution of each tune, when two or more soloist perform, the first soloist will perform his best solo, and the following soloists will perform trying to perform a much better solo, than the previous one, in all of its aspects. In some occasions, it is presented as a "showdown" that occurs, between (among) two or more soloists.

"Jazz is the musical unfolding that can be obtained sometimes inescapably counting on virtuosity, lyricism, and imagination". I imagine the center of the creation/execution of this music, to reside at the intersection of three imaginary planes, that cut the body of the musician. First, it is a vertical plane, placed through the center of the bony marrow (virtuosity), another horizontal plane placed through the heart (lyricism), and a third inclined plane, placed through the brain (creativity by means of the relation of intelligent musical ideas). That intersection would represent the center of (musical) gravity of the musician. Sometimes, while being sad, bored, angry or whatever, not in particular mood for anything, I start listening Jazz, which invariably and immediately, turns my mood into very joyful and pleasant moments. An important variation to Bebop (normal) Jazz, exists when playing blues, supposedly sad ballads, which normally result joyful.

"Scientists are artists and artists are scientists". Absolutely right, my dear Luis Alberto Machado, also I believe that Jazz musicians are artists, and music scientists; they practically are the only musicians that perform experiments, such as: design, improvement and utilization of instruments. Regarding said inventions, modification or utilization only by them, there are; the valve trombone and regarding the modified form of the instrument there are the trumpet utilized by Dizzy Gillespie and Claudio Roditi (CLAUDIO RODITI Y ARTURO SANDOVAL), a rotary valve trumpet, etc. There exists a double bell trumpet, a normal bell and a muted bell utilized by Bobby Shew (BOBBY SHEW HORN).

Regarding the instruments solely utilized by Jazz musicians, we have the vibraphone (vibes) that resembles a marimba which contains vertical resonance tubes placed underneath each key (modern electronic vibes, no longer need them) inside each tube, there are rotating valves (similar to those utilized by carburetors, before the "fuel injection" era). One pedal is provided, in order to have a "sustain" function, that is, to maintain the sound or not of some lately hit note(s).

The sax family, which consists of four main types: soprano, alto, tenor and baritone, all with beautiful timbres, although similar, but all the same, very different.

Some musicians enjoy to sing the corresponding notes and play (such as many bassists, pianists and guitar players), whistle and play guitar (Toots Thielmans), or whistle only (¡but what a way to do it!) as Ron McCroby, who appears in a video mentioned in this book.

Similarly, as there are scientific polymaths, regarding Jazz, there is a very frequent trait, as there exist musicians that master a family of instruments, such as sax players, or such as a trumpet player that can also play a fluegelhorn (same family), which is not easy, since each instrument has its own peculiarities, but nonetheless are somewhat similar. The cited musicians, although they can play any of the instruments of that family, in general, they specialize in only one on them, and only in rare occasions they play some other instrument of the family. Nevertheless, there exist very many virtuous musicians that master several instruments of totally different families such as:

Ron McCroby: clarinet and Puccolo (whistle), Toots Thielmans: guitar (whistling or not) or harmonic. From the super Canadian band of the late Rob McConnell; Don Thomson who recorded one album playing drums, another playing bass, and still another playing piano. Michel Le Grand; pianist, composer, arranger, singer, band director, Bud Shank flautist, alto sax and baritone, Bob Cooper Oboe and tenor sax. Bob Florence; pianist composer, arranger, band conductor, Bill Holman with similar features, except that he plays tenor sax. André Previn Jazz and classical pianist, and orchestra conductor. It is said that; Bob Enevoldsen could play any instrument, etc.

Maynard Ferguson, master high note trumpet player, with an astounding technique, that if not invented by him, was the most well known top performer, who also, played trombone, as well as, many other brass instruments. Arturo Sandoval, the extraordinary Cuban trumpet player that can play even higher notes, as can be seen and heard in a video presented herein.

Polymath classical musicians very possible exist, but until very recently, I had not known any such extraordinary performer, but I now know, at least, one of them: Julia Fisher who plays the Tchaikovsky *violin concerto and* the Griegg *piano concerto* with outstanding performances. Bravo, finally a woman come to the scene.

The problem is in the playing, as well an in its conception, I believe that this assertion, does apply strictly to Jazz music, given that, "that" solo is being conceived, in that precise moment, and there is no margin whatsoever for error of any kind, doubt, or any other type of mistake, and that the creativity most emerge at maximum capacity. Therefore, because of the very same reason, the problem *resides* in playing it, as well as in the complexity of conceiving it.

Following are comments to the book: *La Revolución de la Inteligencia*, by Luis Alberto Machado: "The instrument can be played by anybody, with the intellect only the great creators". This assertion results even more verifiable for the Jazz musicians, due to the "real time", where solos are developed. A painter, or a sculptor, can work "indefinitely", before presenting his work. He can repeat it, correct it, modify his conception, etc. The Jazz musician presents his work "live" (or recording it), without any tolerance for errors, doubts, or corrections, of any kind. The Jazz musician is always on the "knife edge", especially while playing his solo.

"When (a Jazz musician) is going to create, he depends exclusively in his intellect, no other decision than to complete his solo, and no other resource, that his virtuosity".

Another very important area where the Jazz musicians become researchers, similar to scientists, becomes evident with relation to the profound "exploration" of their respective instruments. For example, the discovery of undreamed high notes for a trumpet, as above mentioned. Or the possibility of acquiring unprecedented playing speed (quite frequently in unison) specially while improvising, such as the "marvel" Marian Petrescu presented already in a video. Of course, mere speed, is of no consequence or value, were it is not due to perfection, beauty and lyrical approach, of the so called: "Horowitz" of Jazz.

"Before solving a problem, the problem has to be solved". Otherwise, how can be explained that a virtuoso Jazz musician, can develop his solo, and terminate it with a harmonic, melodic and rhythmic perfection, in the correct bar, and with an appropriate note (with a resolved cord). In order to ground this assertion, I am going to borrow a small portion of an interview, taken from "Jazz wax", to tenor sax player Dave Pell: describing the virtuosity of trumpet player Don Fagerquist: "When Don would start a solo, he knew exactly where he was going to end. He`d would work it out in advance in his head. Then he would play it right up to that ending, that he had in mind, and always wrap his solo on the note he chose". I totally agree. Nevertheless, I insist that, all or most, of the great Jazz virtuosos, are able to accomplish exactly that prodigious feat.

Some Jazz musicians are also, great classical musicians, evidently with utmost perfection such as: Wynton Marsalis, Hubert Laws, Keith Jarret, Chick Corea, etc.

Being one of the main themes of this book music, with respect to classical music, with all the respect that I have for it, and that it deserves, as the source and basis of all cultured music, in my view, the concert musicians, extraordinary and virtuous as they undoubtedly are, are "mere" interpreters, because their creativity is practically restricted, due to the fact that the "best performer", is the one that "captures the spirit and intention of the composer", being the composer the one and only one that carries the glory of the *creativity* of said composition. Yes, I know that are better versions of any piece of music, but again, they are only "better interpretations" Thus, true creativity, in the performer performance, is left basically, to the Jazz virtuosos.

Jerry Coker coments:

"It seems to exist a myth for classical musical as well as for Jazz, that such music genres are created from heavenly inspiration, without control whatsoever from the perfomer and that therefore, intelligence is completlty disconnected from a true artistic creation." The good Jazz musicians, from around the 60's, generally began learning music at a very early age, being this classic music. Later, once theory and the selected instrument were mastered, they initiated their Jazz carrier. Without a doubt, the Jazz musician is an anxious person, who loves to express his personality, his musical style, and his "musical ideas". It is neither sufficient to him, nor interesting, to remain exclusively "inside" of classic music, where in spite of its quality and beauty, an almost total "limitation of own musical expression exists". It is to say, in classical music, a given score must be executed, as it is assumed that the composer conceived it.

In my view, Jazz is the only music genre that has the greater arsenal to its disposition, to manage the comforting music to be listened, from the point of view of variety, it is a vehicle of joy, and a satisfactor of the intellect.

Jazz initiates where classic music ends. That is, Jazz is executed similarly considering the same technical bases as classic music (Harmony, Counterpoint), and in addition utilizes a multitude of techniques that elevates it to high altitude, especially by means of the creativity of improvisation of the solos. In classic music, the soloist virtuoso, is admirable by his execution without a doubt, but creativity does not exist, strictly speaking, the creativity originated and finished when the composer finished his work, and framed exactly, how his work should be played.

When in daily life "improvisation" is mentioned, we tend to think about something "prepared on the knees". In other words, the results generally contain serious faults and/or deficiencies.

Now, if the basic characteristic of Jazz resides in improvisation, it could be possible to think: no wonder that it is so difficult to understand, and therefore that people would like it. Could it be that Jazz musicians play; "whatever comes out the instrument", without greater science and no preoccupation to follow some musical rule? But… it happens that the improvisation in Jazz, is totally in opposition, to the normal improvisation of daily life. Except for very rare exceptions, in order to be able to improvise, classical musical training is required which begins very early in life, deep study of extensive musical theory, and practice until obtaining absolute mastery of the instrument, often looking for, and finding new limits to the instrument, it requires a virtuoso.

The Jazz musicians, who are virtuosos, are so, due to his talent (perhaps 10%), and to its work, and dedication (90%). They generally begin the study of a musical instrument as children. They studied and practiced the theoretical bases of classic music, during several years. Already with that preparation, still it is necessary to see, if they have the creative capacity to improvise, and to develop a personal style.

The true difference, is based in the *creativity* produced by either one. The classic musician, has limited himself to repeat, note by note, each written score, he has never taken advantage of the wonder of improvisation, which was invented and mastered by Mozart and apparently, still better by Bach.

In no form, it is my intention to reduce importance, or any other value to the musical, or artistic value of to the classic musicians, but I point out that, arguably, one the of the most important invention of classic musicians (improvisation), was taken by Jazz musicians exclusively, and plainly ignored by the classic musicians.

Ample "anti-monotony" within Jazz, is obtained in addition, by means of: an enormous variety of instruments played by virtuosos, and a great variety of tempos.

Regarding the variety of utilized instruments, all those that participate in classic music, such as:

Brass: Trumpet, Trombone, French Horn, Flute, Piccolo, etc.

Woods: Clarinet, Oboe and Bassoon.

Strings: Bass, Cello and Violin

Piano

Voice(s)

Almost exclusive Jazz instruments: soprano sax, alto sax, tenor sax, and baritone sax, fluegelhorn (similar to the trumpet with a very pleasant, less "bright" sound), Bass Trombone, Bass Clarinet, vibes, harmonica, electrical guitar (I refer solely to "the real" instrument with acoustic box, not to the table with distorter, utilized in pop music), etc.

I am a purist: I consider, that the acoustic instruments, like the piano and bass, are not normally to be replaced by their "equivalent" electrical counterparts. The 4/4 measure is the fundamental tempo.

For my taste, also only in rare exceptions, the mute in a trumpet (or in any brass instrument) seems attractive, providing a "mysterious" mood. Let us consider a similar example: what would you think, if in a concert hall, a fine Gran Concert Steinway piano, instead of having the lid opened, it had it closed and a very heavy blanket placed on top of the cover? Then the sound, "could not come clearly out from the piano", don't you think? This is indeed, one of the reasons why I dislike trumpet player Miles Davies. Except for two records that I have, in which he plays without the mute, which are very good, all others that I know of, he constantly plays muted trumpet.

The tempos used normally in classic music are 4/4 and ¾, in Jazz, in addition are utilized; 2/2, 5/4, 6/4, etc.

The musical associations can be: from only one soloist (recital), duo, trio, quartet, quintet, sextet, septet, octet, tentet,..... band (approximately 13 members) and great band (approximately 18 members or more), etc.

For a motor-race fan, a Grand Prix is the culminating test of this activity. I believe that without a doubt it is, but what is required for this event, to obtain its attractiveness?

"An orchestrated" organization until the last detail

A perfectly level track

The best teams

The best world rims

The best world oils

The best world mechanics

The best world pilots

Etc.

Why should I mention a Grand Prix here? Because to me, it seems to be the musical equivalent, a concert of big band Jazz. The emotion and joy that produces, is hardly produced by any other musical event.

What is it required so that this spectacle manages to be most attractive:

The best world compositions

The best world arrangements

The best world instruments

The best world virtuosos

Notice, that I do not mention, at all, the concert place (building, lights, etc.) Because, even if it is not offered in the best possible place, this happens to be of secondary nature. The musical performance is the important thing, not the "show", that so frequently replaces the quality of presented music.

Luckily, there still are left a few bands, that can be heard in CD's or live presentations.

Speaking of great bands, I consider that the volume to which they are to be listened, must be "sufficient", by the following considerations:

1-. Being the musical bases of Jazz, similar to those of classic music, similar dynamic differences exist, that is to say, they range from pianissimos, to fortissimos. Therefore if the volume is not sufficient, pianissimos will not be able to be listened at all.

2-. Also, for the same reason, within both musical genres, climax moments exist, which by definition, are of greater dynamic intensity, which are to be appreciated.

3-. When "live" music is listened to, it is heard and enjoyed at "sufficient" volume.

4-. If there is no sufficient volume, the bass can hardly be listened to.

5-. The three sections of a band: saxophones, trombones and mainly trumpets "shine", and produce great emotion, specially during passages of great dynamic content (volume).

I meet many people "which like all type of music". That seems as rare to me, as I must seem to them, when I mention that: I only listen good music. I ask myself: could it be somebody that *loves* a Lamborghini, a Ferrari, a Porsche, a Rolls Royce **and** an Edsel **and** a beaten-up VW beetle **and** "a demolished" old SUV? I consider, that the margin of quality, between these vehicles, and good music and the not good music, is comparable.

Does that mean, that I am too "square" ? I sincerely do not think so, because I would change my musical taste immediately, if anybody could show me some type of music that contained characteristics *better*, than those of the music that I like. What types of innovations would have to invent their creators, that do not exist already, or that can be invented within jazz? But mainly, what interesting activity aside from creativity by means of improvisation could be discovered?

Several cases of Jazz musicians exist, that play classical music as well, being the case of Wynton Marsalis arguably the most remarkable. He started to learn to play trumpet when he was twelve years old, he took the challenge seriously and a year later, he had improved considerably. A few years later, his professor tried to discourage him to play and compete for a price, in the New Orleans Philharmonic, by telling him that nobody wants to listen to a black trumpet player, especially if is accompanied by a full orchestra of white musicians. He learned classical music, that scared black musicians, and found out that it was only more music, and the white musicians were mostly mediocre, and there were very few very good ones. He was able to play twice with that orchestra, and as first trumpet, for the Civic Orchestra of New Orleans, he received the Harvey Shapiro prize for a metal instrument musician. He attended the recognized Julliard music school. He remembers perfectly well, how astonished Gunther Schuller was, when he learned that he also could play Jazz. Given that quality is essencial for him, he has discouraged many musicians to play commercial music, where they have to become clowns, in order to get a job. He always looks sharp on stage.

If I were asked to synthesize in a word the essence of the Jazz, I would think right away about *Creativity*. This creativity can be expressed widely, because improvisation exists. Studying where it occurred for the first time (as mentioned before), we find that improvisation was within the scope of classic music, where this characteristic finds as originators: to Mozart and Bach.

It follows a shorty résumé, from; *Gödel, Escher, Bach*; not other than, Johan Sebastian Bach, probably his inventor, or at least his more capable and more famous performer. There exists an interesting anecdote about Frederic the Great, great king of Prusia (circa 1747), recognized by his high military ability, but a man also dedicated to intelligence and mind. Music was his favorite activity, he was an enthusiastic flutist, and composer and some of his works are interpreted nowadays. Being a protector of arts, he was very attentive to the development of the just created pianoforte (soft-forte). The piano had come evolving during the first half of the XVIII century, as a modified harpsichord. The disadvantage of the harpsichord, was that the volume of the pieces played was uniform, there was no way to play music at different volume ranges. Pianoforte, as it name implies, solved this problem. The Italian, Bartolomeo Cristofori (BARTOLOMEO CRISTOFORI), built the first pianoforte which rapidly began to be wanted everywhere. The German, Gotttfried Silvermann, the best organ constructor, set his mind and body to construct a perfect pianoforte. Evidently, the best help to his tenacity came from the king. It is said that Federico had at least fifteen Silvermann pianos. Federico, admirer of pianos, was also admirer of Bach. Bach's, music was considered by some people as incomprehensible, while others considered them as masterpieces.

What everybody recognized, was Bach's mastery while improvising upon the organ. Federico used to organize musical evenings. Often he himself acted as a soloist, of some flute concerts. In certain occasion, while he was preparing his instrument and his musicians were ready to begin, an assistant gave him the list of foreign guests, and when learning that Johan Sebastian Bach was there, he excused himself in order to receive Bach, as he deserved, by canceling the concert. Followed by his musicians, Federico invited Bach to test each one of his pianos, and to play in them, some improvisations. After testing several pianos, Bach asked the king to provide a theme to him, offering himself to execute it immediately, without any preparation, —that is, improvising upon it—. The king became delighted by the intelligent and beautiful playing, where his proposed theme was utilized as a fugue, and, no doubt, intrigued by how far Bach could improvise, he requested to listen a fugue by six obligated voices. But since not every theme is appropriate for a so rich harmony, Bach himself chose one theme, and with great mastery, he improvised based on it according to the desire of the king. Once back in Leipzig, Bach worked on the subject for the king, and he wrote pieces for three and six voices and he ordered to record his work, with the title; *Musical Offering,* which was dedicated to the original inventor of theme.

The second word, of extreme importance, that defines Jazz, is the very precise rhythm (swing), that it must be maintained, by the soloist, and all other group members. It is the contagious rhythm, that "forces" the listeners to move their feet correspondingly. The rhythm, base of Jazz, is provided by the bass. The drums, provide a rhythm complement (the time), and finally, the piano completes the so called "rhythm section", by means of agreed rhythmic and melodic chords. The bass and the piano are responsible also, "to suggest" chord changes, to the soloists, while performing their solos.

It is extremely common, to find multi-instrumentalists Jazz musicians of the same family of instruments, like for example a sax player, able to virtuously execute anyone of the four types of saxes. These musicians frequently can also play, with the same mastery: clarinet, flute, piccolo, oboe and even bassoon.

There also exist musicians with very special talents, that can improvise a solo in his instrument (guitar) and whistle in unison, his name: Thoots Thielmans. Others can ("sing in scales"), while simultaneously improvising his solo (pianists and bass players).

Brad Mehldau, the extraordinary young pianist, declared a very interesting fact; "If all the charts in the world were reduced to ashes, a concert could be offered that same night, with totally strange musicians and without any rehearsal". By all means, that could be possible only for Jazz musicians. And peculiarly, that could easily be, a memorable concert.

Within art, a copy, even the most perfect one, has little value; (even can, in certain cases, constitute an illicit act) speaking of painting, sculpture and architecture, for example. In particular, when we talk of classical music, the exactly opposite happens. The closer an interpretation is played to the believed "spirit" of the composer, when he conceived it, up to the minimum detail, this execution has value, otherwise, it is of no worth. Personally, I believe that to be correct, but it is an interesting peculiar exception of all other art.

For which reason has the deluxe chimp invented tools (and instruments)? I cannot think about some tool (instrument) that man has invented, since stone age, whose intention has not been to multiply, from a few times, to millions of times which man can do, without using this tool or instrument. The human voice, being something wonderful, −what a different our civilization would be without speech−, but when used to sing, is very limited in many aspects, compared with the amplitude of maneuver of the musical instruments. With few exceptions, the best voices, those that have had years of study and practice to obtain excellence levels, are encountered mainly within classic music.

Since about half of the XX century, and now practically dominating all the musical scope, "vocal pop music", is heard almost without exception in all mass media, films, vehicles public and private, supermarkets, concerts, all type of stores, offices, programs on science, ads, etc., and even in churches.

I believe that this situation presents several situations to consider:

1-. This "sung pop music" has monopolized all the "Hertzian spectrum" (A.M., FM and TV, etc.). Not to mention almost every store, and hallway in every shopping center, as well as, almost every restaurant globally. For me (and surely, for many people), this is totally unacceptable, because all persons that want to hear another type (quality) of music, do not have other alternatives.

2-. I perfectly well understand the cause of this situation, the world-wide population has been conditioned, not only to accept this imposition, they even have become fervently addicted to it.

3-. If this "sung pop music" had, at least, a minimum musical quality, would not be as much damaging. But it happens all the opposite, the most disagreeable and repulsive voices are those most "successful". As well as; teenage voices that are, or at least appear, to be "dumber than hell".

Also, the lyrics of these songs are the most irrelevant, monotonous, and with null imagination, being in great deal, obscene and grotesque.

4-. They promote a terrible example for our youth, that is to say: neither study, nor experience is required. Quality is unthinkable as well as unnecessary in order to become "successful", but rather the opposite. Form your group, buy and wear weird costumes or ridiculous uniforms, and you already constitute possible candidate to attract audiences to fill auditoriums.

5-. Inclusive, at cosmic level, all these waves emitted from Earth, in some years might begin to arrive to other planets that might be inhabited by intelligent beings, which probably will not be interested in contacting us, based on samples of such a poor "civilization".

6-. This monopoly of "sung popular music", witch certainty has caused that an enormity of instrument musicians, with enormous potential anywhere in the world, have changed their musical inclinations probably towards other professions or activities that allowed them, a "modus vivendi" acceptable to them. The amount of "wasted" virtuoso talent, probably could amount to several thousand. Survival of professional Jazz musicians is really tough.

I have encountered something very strange: until not too long ago, the music heard by "folk people", like clerks, construction workers, public transport drivers, etc., almost exclusively consisted of: "folk *local* artists", that is to say: Mexican music. Almost suddenly, now all this people listen to American pop music, which most of them do not even understand (the stupid nonsense, that it is being sung). How was it possible to change their several decades of existent tradition, in such a short time? How can they constantly hear something that, it is totally unintelligible to them?

The lack of appreciation of instrumental music is already several decades old. I remember the film; "Man with a Horn" staring Kirk Douglas, in the roll of a trumpet player, who asks with sadness to his friend musician, why is that his music does not please audiences, that he thinks that it should? His friend replies to him, that is because; "the audiences like extremely simple monotonous songs, that they themselves can sing".

It is peculiar that new technology was the main cause by which Jazz continued to lose followers. At the time when 78 RPM records were around, the duration of each track was between 3 and 4 minutes. Of this time, 1 minute was used for the outset playing the melody theme, and another minute at the end of the tune. One to two minutes were utilized for improvising the solo(s). The replacing acetate technology of 33 RPM LP `s, the magnetic tapes and the CD's, where the soloist could expand each solo, several minutes more. This allowed each soloist to develop a solo, not only of much greater duration, but much more interesting, requiring much greater musical and intellectual capacity. Unfortunately, this same benefit for the Jazz lover, moved away immense amounts of previous Jazz fans, that no longer were able to understand, the increased beauty of the extended solos.

In another film (by Walt Disney), of which I do not remember its name, the main protagonist, is a young man who has as his assistant a chimpanzee. The job of this young person consists, of finding "new musical values". The work of the assistant chimp, consists of choosing between several groups, the group that presumably will be a success. The assistant was an "infallible genius" in his work. The film results very entertaining, by the performance and the commercial aptitude of the chimp. Probably this is not the real form, in which it is determined a group as successful (but it could easily be). But sincerely I do not believe that the chimpanzee had such a bad ear and taste, to choose with precision the success of modern groups, rather he knew, the awful taste of their cousins, the deluxe chimps. In one book (by Dr. Sagan?), I remember to have read the mention: that chimps preferred Jazz to pop music.

When I was an adolescent, I liked to read "MAD" magazine. In one of those magazines that I still keep: (The ninth Annual edition of more trash from MAD), appears a department: "Mad's teenager idol promoter of the year". It seems to me that, at least when I used to read this magazine, it truly had articles of a genius and excellent sense of humor. The department mentioned here seems to me as one of their best. The strategy used in this writing refers to finding a musical idol, is apparently improbable, because it arrives to an impressive absurd level, but given what it is heard today, that must indeed be the strategy used at the present time. It goes like this: a reporter interviews a pop music promoter of "new values". When looking both of them thru a window, they observe a complete jerk that causes pity to see, and another clean young teenager who displayed good attitude, with books under the arm, and that has all the appearance of being a healthful boy, in all the extension of the word. The promoter comments to the reporter; that he can turn the young fellow into a "star" very quickly. The reporter agrees that indeed the young good looking boy could have talent to cultivate, to which the promoter responds to him: no, I am talking about the other fellow (the jerk). To prepare the good looking, will take me some days, with the bum, four hours will be enough. Then, the interview continues with a very important test, to determine the probability of success of the new singer, constitutes the hearing of a prospect before a group of family parents. If parents like the new singer, he is automatically discarded, It implies that he is not "sufficiently annoying" to the parents. Finally, the selected prospect shown is; "Salt Simeon", a gorilla that will surely be a great sensation.

But this is hardly a joke which has lasted more than fifty years and the level of absurdity, monotonous, grotesque and vulgarity continues advancing to unsuspected levels, the situation is truly worrisome.

In the United States, the invention of Jazz took place, event which I personally consider of a cultural importance of first magnitude. It is important to mention, that this type of music has been the only really important contribution of the United States in the scope of the arts, at least with reference to music. That is: *Jazz is the Classical Music of the United States*.

I cannot think about some other example of a country that produces the best product of some type, and the worse one of that same type of product. Reason why I reach the following conclusion: In the United States, the best music (Jazz) was invented, as well as, the "*best* anti-music" (rock and similar garbage).

"MAKING" MONEY AND MAKING MUSIC

This it is the title of an essay written by Tommy Vig in 1977, *who appears in the back cover of the LP "ENCOUNTER WITH TIME", produced by Discovery Record #DS780.* This paper was rejected for publication by; the "New York Times", "Newsweek", and "Psychology Today"; portions of said essay follow, in my own words:

Vig was very surprised about the public feeling about the death of Elvis Presley, and he felt obligated to express his point of view, as that of a professional U.S. musician. For him, Elvis was an unprepared, musically untrained young truck driver, with no musical abilities whatsoever. But notably, his shows were viewed and heard by multitude of youngsters. The implications were very preoccupating indeed: that you did not have to have musical talent and regardless you could become famous and rich. To be at the top without really trying. It represented a symbol of money, which has been the supreme value of our society. If millions of youngsters will pay to hear him, he must be good (for money making, not music). At first, some of us thought that it was only a bad joke, that it would go away any minute.

But it was good music or good money? The difference is important. Is it bad music harmful for the intellect in the same form that some foods (white sugar) are harmful for the body? The Beatles did not know anything about music. They would never had been admitted to a reasonable conservatory even at the level of students, since they did not have the most minimal musical talent, elementary discipline or training. But, one thing is to have fun and circus, but to proclaim these poor unprepared amateur kids without talent as great musical figures, is another very different subject. Tommy Vig's, especialty and his sphere of knowledge is music, but he feels that by observing the commercial exploitation in music is a reflection in the attitudes of the society in general. In the musical industry of today, the majority is the ONLY judge. By todays standards, good music means money producing music. For most people, good music is what they like. Next

Searching for a less subjective yardstick to measure the quality of music, he looked for the registries of successes (hits) of the two previous decades. It was very difficult for him, to find several musical pieces of serious quality among them, and none of them corresponds to artists like; Rachmaninoff, Chet Baker, Beethoven, Bob Florence, Shorty Rogers, etc. In effect, no true classical work or creation of Jazz ever becomes a "hit".

This observation, reaches the inevitable conclusion that, it is extremely unlikely, that music of great quality, may be liked by the majority of people. Rather, it seems to be that, popular music is so different from the music of great quality, that calling "music" to both, is, by all means, incorrect. The writers and performers must be formed by youngsters with neither musical talent, nor musical training, white men, appareled with strange uniforms and behaving in extremely erratic and childish form. The guys utilize primitive harmonies, melodies and rhythm, that show an exceptional lack of imagination, lack of rhythm, and express crude and infantile emotions. They have very few performers, with a very reduced kind of instruments, mainly the hideous electric guitar and, of course, the extremely noisy drums. The singers seem to be chosen out from the worst and most horrible and childish existing voices.The number of people to whom they like does not determine its inherent value. Music is created to be the best possible, probably not necessarily the most saleable one, and there are no restrictions with respect to the age or genre of the executants, its number, so long as they are individuals with formal or informal training and artistic commitment, and are individuals with musical talent. The variety of harmonies, melodies, rhythms, tempos, instrumentation, color, orchestration, dynamics and range of expression are limited solely by the imagination.

This leads to Vig's possible formula to measure the quality of music: "IF A LARGE NUMBER OF PEOPLE LIKE IT, IT IS MORE THAN LIKELY, OF LOW QUALITY". In other words, in general, the quality of music is inversely proportional to the percentage of populace which likes it.

The reverse of it, of course, is not true, the: "LACK OF SUCCESS OF TODAY'S MUSIC, AUTOMATICALLY DOES NOT MEAN THAT IT IS GOOD".

In his opinion (and mine also), people should be free to hear what they like, as they are in a free country. Unfortunately, at the moment; "the musical taste of the majority, is the only measurement that applies to the broadcasters, and disc manufacturers, when they decide on the product. In the process, they avoid that many radio listeners have variety and choice. They leave ALL individuals to ONLY what the majority wants to listen.

Tommy Vig is an orchestra conductor, arranger, and vibes player; he knows what he is talking about.

In fact, the above formula, I believe that applies to almost everything, that is of the liking of populace, with respect to sports, political parties, and what have you.

Given the "freedom of expression" that it is assumed to exists in the United States, this essay called my attention strongly. Three of the most important newspapers and magazines did not dare (or was inconvenient for them) to publish this document? What relation had or have with the "entertainment" mafias? Everything aims at that, if they are not the owners or partners, they protect them very well.

A scene of a very good old film (long ago, when I still used to go to the cinema) called; "Soylent Green" starring Charlton Heston and Edward G. Robinson, impressed me. Edward G. Robinson, who is about to die, requests that he is permitted to lie down in a comfortable reclining armchair, before a great screen to see and listen to landscapes and beautiful classic music and to extinct animals due to human destruction. Its excellent performance reveals its ecstasy when contemplating the beautiful animals, recoverable only in photography, no longer in the real life. I experiment myself a similar scene very frequently. A difference exists, it does not happen to me before a cinematographic projection, but before an exquisite art, as it is Jazz music. The experience starts while listening a type of music that miraculously has resisted extinction (so far), not by cause of Greenpeace, but due to a few musicians and some remaining few enthusiasts of the good music mentioned in this book. Thus, I accommodate myself in a comfortable reclining sofa, that I enjoy, with similar ecstasy, when listening the wonderful music created by extremely intelligent virtuoso musicians. When closing my eyes, I can imagine, very clearly, the performers of such wonder. When listening to an orchestra (big band), for example, I can perfectly visualize, each section as they interact: trumpets, saxes and trombones, to each soloist and the other members of the band. It seems to me incredible, that this great musical genre is near extinction. As incredible as the animal extinction, like the wonderful tiger, for example. Luckily, still a few musicians exist, in many countries, that refuse to let Jazz die, this fantastic art form, that demands a matchless unfolding of virtuosity, sensitivity, creativity, imagination, good taste and intelligence that it is tending to be extinguished.

SIX

WORLD-WIDE REJECTION TO THE PROPOSED METHOD

"I am not pessimistic, to perceive evil where it exists,
it is in my opinion, an optimism form"
Roberto Rosellini

Long before writing this book, I have asked myself the possible veracity in regard to a well-known popular belief that says; "One of the main preoccupations of almost all governments, has been and it is, to make sure that the immense majority of their citizens remain intellectually passive (stupid), because such large crowds are easy to manipulate". Since a theory, without testing does not have practical use, I decided to test it as follows: I personally delivered letters directed to twelve of the most powerful nations on Earth. Presumably, also the most cult. In these letters (a copy is included in this book), I asked for an appointment, directly with the respective ambassador; the idea was to present him a: "Method to improve Intelligence" of children and adolescents dramatically, which I discovered after years of reflection, and which already I described, in detail, in a previous chapter.

It was evident their total lack of interest since *none* of these embassies ever sent a received acknowledgment or an answer letter, even if it was a refusal to grant an appointment. The elementary politeness to reply a received letter no longer exists, even in the embassies of the most powerful countries on earth?

Next I present a copy of the original letter sent to those embassies:

Entre-ligare

Improvement of Intelligence

EMBASSY OF ▇▇▇▇

Mr. ▇▇▇▇▇▇

Honorable Ambassador

Julio 10/03

Subject: Intensive intelligence improvement in your country.

Honorable Ambassador:

I am writing and directly addressing this letter to your kind attention, because I believe it refers to a matter of vital importance, to the important country which you represent in Mexico, and I want to make sure that you receive this information.

I think that I have conceived a method that will allow your country, to educate at high level, a large number of its inhabitants, in the most important, distinctive human activity and most pressing ever, even for the survival of our species in the 21st. century. As you surely know, one of the most pressing scientific warnings, is the conclusion of the book published by the Club of Rome titled: "The Predicament of Mankind", and latter: "The Limits to Growth" by Donella and Dennis Meadows from the MIT.

It is truly alarming the scarce use of intelligence shown at worldwide level. I propose that the said method should apply (as compulsory material) starting at the beginning of primary school (at the latest) and continue until there is a total mastering of this method. Consistently, it should carry out a comprehensive review of the rest of the subjects taught during each school year.

With this scheme, I think possible to prepare a significant number of professionals, especially prominent scientists in several areas (in English "polymath"), i.e., having many "generalists" instead of specialists.

It is important to note that, as that whatever is really worthwhile in life, an important and continuous effort is needed to achieve this. It also requires investment in the form of study materials, training of teachers and the cost of this method. The benefit to your country could be enormous.

Being this an innovative concept, there will very probably be initial resistance. I sincerely hope that this time, this is not the case. I also hope that I have managed to interest you, so you may like to learn more about this proposal. The survival issue mentioned above, does not refer to persons unknown for centuries to come, almost surely is referring to our children and grandchildren.

Gladly, I would like to expand on details, if you will allow me the honor by providing an appointment to talk about said subject.

I look forward to your kind reply.

Sincerely

Ing. José Octavio Velasco

solar@prodigy.net.mx
5374-1160 04455- 7141-26-66

Given the novelty of my idea and its "vehicle", I feel that it would be a difficult uphill task, but I hope that my book is taken seriously, that it deserves a very ample and worldwide try. After all, the future of our children and grandchildren is at stake. Our predicament is *our*, it is not risking the generations of unknown people. Wake up. Last Call.

I mentioned above that in Venezuela, during the mandate of President Luis Herrera Camping, Dr. Luis Alberto Machado was named *Secretary of State for the Development of Intelligence*. As a conclusive demonstration of my above mentioned thesis, the "Secretary for the Development of Intelligence" was dismantled immediately when the following government of Venezuela took possession. No other such government agency has ever been created elsewhere, neither in Venezuela nor in any other country. Does any doubt remains on this matter?

What opposition, disadvantages and difficulties can appear before accepting, and during application of the suggested method? This method can be adopted from school level, city level, country level or world-wide level.

Opposition. Like any new idea or innovative proposal, it would not surprise me that the initial reaction, is of doubt as far as their expected results, and it even could be of frank ridicule and/or rejection. If the initial reaction is of doubt, it seems excellent to me, because it would reveal (at least, apparently), that the scientific method would have been applied, at least, with respect to skepticism. If the process stops there, I would see it very deplorable, since I believe that sufficient and necessary arguments exist that deserves it to be *"proven"*, among other things; so that this suggestion is considered seriously, and that is fulfilled by a verification that allows to measure qualitative and quantitatively its benefits, or the lack of them. If a frank rejection exists, without greater study, −a priori−, bad news for all, we will continue the accelerated degradation and destruction towards civilization type − 1 (barbarism).

Some of the possible disadvantages (referring to time, effort and money), on the part of the possible interested ones before accepting the application of the "Relational Linkage" (called: "Method of Relation" by Dr. Machado) that I anticipate that they can have are the following:

a. Possible resistance to review and to modify the syllabus, so that the improvement of intelligence could be really obtained, and contributes to live more complete lives in all aspects, lived with wisdom.

b. Possible resistance of some parents to understand and to accept, the positive consequences of this method, and to want to make an effort to provide the required atmosphere, in agreement with the scholastic plan, to manage a propitious familiar atmosphere, in order to obtain the goal, mentioned in the previous paragraph.

c. Resistance from companies, mass media, entertainment and governments to the "generalized adoption" of this method, because they fear that it will affect their interests.

d.   I believe that probably a very important initial resistance would arise from some schools, some parents and some children and teenagers, that could argue that; "from where will it come the time" for the study of music, science and moral values?

My answer is that it can come from three places: a better syllabus, more time for classes (in Korea, China, etc., schools do it and nothing happens, other than accelerated progress), and finally and extremely important item, the time wasted watching TV and the unsettling mad, violent video games that can free time, so it can be utilized to take advantage of the mentioned activities. We know that according to the saying; "there is no free lunch", that which is really "worth the trouble" obviously has a cost, and the more worth, the more effort is required.

In order to corroborate what a quality education offers, I will take a small fragment of an interview that Gunther Schuller gave to "Jazz Wax"; "I was a mischievous and rebel child, so my parents sent me to a very strict German school... I had an incredible education. During the second year, I studied subjects suchs as: French, Latin, Geography and Geology... I had a serious accident with a knive, where I lost my right eye, and my mother had to go get me, in order to send me to New York. There I studied in another private school – St. Thomas Choir School -. That school was almost as rigorous as the German one, so I had little time for other things, other than studying. What I am now, is due, in grand part, to the education received in Germany and New York".

Very probably difficulties, predicted and not anticipated could arise (referring to time, effort and money), if the suggested method got to be adopted. Frankly, I do not believe that any of them is really insurmountable. Given the expected benefit, I believe that it is worth the trouble to plan, at least the majority of these, to anticipate by means of practical and intelligent solutions. Given the sad present situation, the even sadder foreseeable near future, if the suggested method could obtain, a small percentage of success (considering a good number of participants), it would be criminal to discard it without testing it. If the suggested method has the possibility, say in 20 years, "to produce"; a Newton, or a Leonardo, or an Einstein, to name some really shining men who contributed invaluable knowledge to our civilization, would it not be worth the trouble, and all the required effort?

DIAGRAM OF SUGGESTED CIVILIZATION
DESPERATELY NEEDED BASED IN *SAPIENS* HOMO

Possible profit: World-wide mental reversion tending to good sense

Globalized Planet earth with intelligence and justice, changes such as:

Expedite action on: "Limits to Growth" recommendations

Generalized correct use of science and the Scientific Method

Nations/industries worried about a finite planet

Marketing limited in volume, intelligent and truthful

To be, is the important thing in life, to *have* is a secondary priority

Healthy mind in healthy body

Creative entertainment

The suggested: "Relational Linkage" implemented worldwide

Peak oil and climate change taken seriously

Etc.

INPUT

⇩

BRAINS (Hardware)

⇩

Intelligent concepts ⇨ PROCESS ⇨ Many more
intelligent concepts

⇩

OUTPUT

The improvement of Intelligence, applied with wisdom,
might allow the survival of our species and it could allow
civilizations type I, and above in a distant future

STABLE CYLINDER
Explanation of the diagram.

The quick, deep, enthusiastic, intelligent, and globalized application of the "Relational Linkage", with the suggested complementary additional changes (and surely many others) proposed in this book can presumably obtain the mental reversion to prudence, that could allow the survival of our *new conceptual species:* "Sapiens homo" (intelligence would control the animal, not the other way around like nowadays).

In this way, the INPUT consisting of multiple positive and intelligent activities in the brain, will produce its intelligent process, while the OUTPUT, will allow the improvement of the intelligence, applied with wisdom, that might allow the survival of our species and hopefully could allow civilizations type I, II and III in the distant future.

Our survival depends on this change. In addition, in which other form the types of civilizations I, II and III can be conceived?

I believe that this upgrade can be obtained. Let us see, each one of us have his/her own supercomputer −our brain−. The wonderful existing computers, at the present time, exceed some of our capacities in inconceivable magnitudes (and every day they will be better). Nevertheless, with all probability, they will never be able to think "freely", that is its more serious borderline (by definition, they are programmed) and also constitutes our greater advantage.

However, the computers improve, by improving the computer in itself (hardware) and/or the operating systems (i.e. Windows) and other programs (i.e. Word and Exel). Since the human beings already have a supercomputer (hard to improve), what we can and we must improve is our "operating system" (our software). Which is the only and evident form to improve it? By means of the education of human beings in integral form, with improvement of our intelligence and wisdom, by utilizing: a "Relational Linkage" described in detail already in this book.

EPILOGUE

I really hope that this book has a great international interest. This interest not necessarily will prove immediately positive, because all innovating idea, almost invariably, is difficult to accept. The only thing that would bother me worse and even would sadden me, is that it passed inadvertent, as already happened in the twelve mentioned embassies. This would indicate, at least for me, that hardly would be hope, because due to inertia, we will run out of time. That for some reason, the people, mainly those that can take decisions at various levels: state, national or international, do not want to realize our predicament, or they are so egoistic that they are not interested in their life, or the life of their children and grandchildren.

I have dedicated myself with true passion, enthusiasm, and dedication, during several years to write this book, because I have very deep interest for my family, my country and the world where we live. Although, in the final account, really it would not matter, it would please me to have belonged to a winning team, that is, to a civilization that did not, very stupidly self-destructed itself, but rather to one that had advanced until reaching a level of civilization I (at least).

Without doubt, I can be mistaken, the suggested method might not produce the result foretold. Since I have spoken here, and I am convinced, of the validity of the scientific method, the first thing that I request, is that, if it is doubted the effectiveness of the "Relational Linkage" (hypothesis) here proposed, the second thing that I request, is that it is scientifically tested, with sufficiency, and established with the sufficient time required, so that are its qualitative and quantitative benefits favor it, or if not, to be discarded by the lack of them.

This book consists of two main areas.

The first area concerns science. Without any doubt, we would continue to be not even deluxe chimps, but rather cave men, had not been thanks to science, so let's give science its proper dimension. Science has been wrongly utilized many times, but what has not? I do not believe that anything exists, where the deluxe chimp has not, in a short while has found an evil, vulgar, damaging, etc., use of it. The example that currently amazes me the most is the Internet. Such communication marvel, immediately started to get full of garbage of all kinds. But what about the immensity volume of "worms and viruses" appearing every day? There are two possible culprits: if produced by the "virus protecting companies", it is a shame and a crime, but if produced by hackers, which utilize their clever minds to cause serious damage to potentially *millions of unknown people*, what is inside of their skulls?

The second area is concerned with my proposed: "Relational Linkage". As I presented three "demonstrations" that the proposed "Method of Relation" as suggested by Dr. Luis Alberto Machado, applied to learning Jazz music, with the intention of becoming a virtuoso (or as close as possible), has great probability to constitute a very appropriate approach, to increase significantly the intelligence of the human race. But let's assume, that after trying in depth, and with "sufficiently" wide span, the results are not important, at least many people would have access to Jazz, and would provide them with invaluable happiness, for the rest of their lives, listening to a genre that hardly would have been known to them otherwise, given the almost null promotion it receives.

So, what then, in my opinion, is the purpose of life of the deluxe chimp? Clearly, the "point of view" of nature (evolution), is to try to survive (long enough) – in order to reproduce as much as possible– (the catholic church and other religions, blindly promoting it) which is demonstrated by the ever growing human population. Evidently, this is also the behavior of the ordinary deluxe chimp.

A "proper" deluxe chimp, which utilizes his thinking capacity sufficiently, will take care to have only one small family, where each child will have the best available resources (material & intellectual), as well as, dedicated time, so he/she can grow into a wise individual. I also believe that the purpose of life, with respect to the "spiritual" sense, it is to learn, as much as possible, about the working of the Cosmos (science), if not as a professional scientist, at least as an amateur, so the "Pleasure of Finding Things Out" of Richard Feynman fills your life. If you allow elderly people to pass their experience to you: exercise sufficiently, eat good food (not fattening), do not have any kind of vice and listen, as much as you can, good Jazz, I believe that you can live a happy life.

At the latest part of my life, I was able to write five books, about my passions, which gave me, great pleasure. Also, to live very near to the end of the interval of industrialization, as to all those who are alive now, and the very few generations that could follow us, because, among other sensational events we had to see:

The short cosmic adventure, including missions to the Moon, Mars, other planets and travel outside of our solar system.

The Hubble Space Telescope (et al.) that provided us with absolutely stunning images of the universe (not simply the "firmament").

The completed human genome project.

Medical advances, without one of which I would not be alive today (angioplasty).

Advances in engineering and architecture, in all aspects.

Etc.

The only "discrepancy" that I had, with respect to my children, is that, I would have loved that they had acquired my tastes, not only because they are my tastes, but rather basically because I consider them to be very worthwhile. Take for example, Jai Alai as the sport to practice during your life. Regarding music, how about Jazz and classical music, to please your ears and intellect? And finally how about becoming interested in science (even only at amateur level) to learn about how the cosmos "works", and thus become skeptical, so that we are not easily fooled? Is there anything wrong with any of them? Unfortunately, I was unable to guide my children into the mentioned "marvel" areas. The mass media and their "peers" resulted much more convincing than I.

Nobody likes to be mistaken, but with respect to my fears with respect to the predicted possible outcome, I hope to be completely mistaken, since my children and their children could live indescriptible hardships. They are not interested, or plainly they do not believe the warnings regarding the predicament they will directly face, and therefore they are not aware of the minimum surviving measures to be taken, such as: learn permaculture (SURVIVAL GARDENING PEAK

OIL FOOD STORAGE), look for an "adequate" place where to live when the "Post carbon" era arrives (TIIE LONG EMERGENCY), (THE END OF SUBURVIA), etc.

The third Chimpanzee by Jared Diamond, mentions: that within the last few decades, we have developed the means to send radio signals to other stars and also to blow ourselves any moment. Even if we don`t come to that quick end, our harnessing of much of the earth`s productivity, our extermination of species, and our damage to the environment are accelerating at a rate that cannot be sustained for even another century. As more countries with devastating more power fight for fewer resources, something catastrophic will happen. There are reasons to be very preoccupied. Even if every human living today, were to die tomorrow, the damage that we already have done to our environment, due to inertia, would cause that its degradation will continue for decades.

That pessimistic view is captured in a sentence by the Dutch explorer Arthur Wichmann, which devoted a decade of his life, to write on the history of New Guinea exploration. He grew disillusioned as he realized that successive explorers committed the same stupidities, again and again….The bitter last sentence of the last volume was; "¡Nothing learned, and everything forgotten!" I am afraid that, that very alarming phrase does not apply only to New Guinea explorers, but rather to the global population in general. Regarding, what I believe to be my area of expertise, where I need to learn about the Jazz musicians accomplishments, I become very angry and sad, time and time again, with some exceptions, when I read about the short, dramatic, traumatic, tragic and absolutely stupid untimely decline of the astonishing intellect and mastering of instruments of most of the "Greats". Why should I become angry and sad, no one were relatives or even friends? Well, because one of the most crucial ambition in my life, was to become a virtuoso Jazz trumpet musician, which I could not because of lack of talent and problems of embouchure, and these gifted marvels end up in the gutter, by self determination, at the peak of their life. Is it not the more shameful, absurd and stupid behavior?

How is it possible that they repeat exactly the fatal faults of their pears? How is it possible that they could ever "taste" any drug, even once? Again; "¡Nothing learned, and everything forgotten!"

And I dare to postulate a new law, as true and valid, as any of the conservation laws of physics, coining the title: "Law of Conservation of Stupidity of the deluxe chimp", for all human civilizations (so far), culminating with our global version, that sooner or later could become extinct, sincerely hoping to be dead wrong.

Finally, the "enhanced" intelligence either achieved by the "Relational Linkage" described within this book (or any other method), that is not taken intensively, immediately and worldwide, will be crucial for the coming decades. Because if we do not achieve this goal very fast, probably: ¡goodbye deluxe chimps! And if that happens, my appreciation of our species, and the title of this book should have been: "*Damn ape stupidly clever*".

YOUTUBE videos

(DENNIS MEADOWS – ECONOMICS AND LIMITS TO GROWTH (3))

(THE POLITICAL MOTIVATIONS BEHIND THE ORCHESTRATION OF 9/11).

(JANE GOODALL – OVERPOPULATION IN THE DEVELOPING WORLD)

(WORLD OVERPOPULATION AWARENESS)

(THE HUMAN OVERPOPULATION CRISIS)

(THE MOST TERRIFYING VIDEO YOULL EVER SEE)

(HOW IT ALL ENDS: INDEX)

(RICHARD HEIBERG PEAK OIL)

(MATT SIMMONS PEAK OIL)

(PAT MURPHY PEAK OIL)

(COLIN CAMPBELL, PEAK OIL)

(MIKE RUPERT PEAK OIL & COLLAPSE)

(DR, PETER LLOYD PEAK OIL)

(RICHARD HEIMBERG PEAK EVERYTHING (6 PARTS)).

(THE END OF SUBURBIA) (THE LONG EMERGENCY).

(RICHARD HEINBERG THE POLITICAL MOTIVATIONS BEHIND THE ORCHESTRATION OF 9/11)

(EVIDENCE THAT GEORGE W. BUSH HAD ADVANCED KNOWLEDGE)

(THE BEST 9/11 DOCUMENTARY)

(SCHOLARS FOR 9/11 THRUTH)

(9/11 TOTAL PROOF THAT BOMBS WERE PLACED IN THE BUILDINGS)

(ZEITGEIST, THE MOVIE, FINAL EDITION)

(9-11 BLUEPRINT FOR TRUTH (13 parts))

(RETIRED EXPERT PILOT JOHN LEAR- NO PLANES HIT THE TOWERS)

(MAYNARD FERGUSON 1977 CLINIC)

(MAYNARD FERGUSON CLINIC:01. A BRIEF SERMON)

(LEE RITENOUR WITH BRIAN BROMBERG STOLEN MOMENTS)

(WILLIE MAIDEN IMPROV MUSIC CLINIC)

(PAUL DESMOND PLAYS "EMILY")

(GEORGE SHEARING I`LL BE AROUND)

(DAVE BRUBECK - TAKE THE "A TRAIN 1966)

(MICHEL PETRUCCIANI & TRIO – BITE)

(MARCIAL SOLAL GREEN DOLPHIN STREET)

(OSCAR & ANDRE PLAY TOGETHER)

(OSCAR PETERSON & MICHEL LEGRAND IN SHOW)

(MARIAN PETRESCU-CARAVAN)

(STAN GETZ-GREEN DOLPHIN STREET)

(DYLAN`S DELIGHT PEPPER ADAMS)

(CARMEN McRAE SINGS I`M GLAD THERE IS YOU)

(THE FOUR FRESHMEN – POINCIANA)

(ANDY MARTING SOLOING ON A MINOR AFFAIR)

(FRANK ROSOLINO ITALY 1970`S W/CONTE CANDOLY)

(FRANK ROSOLINO & RAUL DE SOUZA – CORCOVADO)

(DEXTER GORDON - GREEN DOLPHIN STREET)

(SELLY MANNE QUARTET – BLUES IMPROVISATION)

(CLIFFORD BROWN & MAX ROACH JOY SPRING)

(LEE MORGAN I REMEMBER CLIFFORD)

(FREDDY HUBBARD JOY SPRING)

("AUTUMN LEAVES" CHET BAKER – PAUL DESMOND)

(RED RODNEY – HOW DO YOU KNOW)

(SHORTY ROGERS & HIS GIANTS INFINITE PROMENADE)

(WYNTON MARSALIS - MOTO PERPETUO)

(GEORGE COLLEMAN & AHMED JAMAL MY FOOLISH HEART)

(RON MCCROBY EL MEJOR SILBADOR DEL MUNDO)

(DAVID PERRICO MY FOOLISH HEART)

(BIG BAND OF LISZT BLUE DANIEL)

(WOODY HERMAN REUNION AT NEWPORT)

(PORTLAND JAZZ ORCHESTRA – QUINCY JONES - STOCKHOLM SWEETENING)

(DOUBLE SIX OF PARIS STOCKHOLM SWEETENING)

(ROB MCCONNELL STREET OF DREAMS)

(STAN KENTON ARTISTRY IN RHYTHM (9))

(STAN KENTON MY OLD FLAME)

(BILL HOLMAN KINGFISH)

(BILL HOLMAN THEME IN VARIATIONS)

(BOB FLORENCE CARMELO`S BY THE FREEWAY THE BOB FLORENCE LIMITED EDITION)

(BOB FLORENCE A TRIBUTE TO BOB FLORENCE)

(GRP ALL STAR BIG BAND BLUE TRAIN)

(GRP ALL STAR BIG BAND CHEROKEE)

(LA JAZZ INST. CARL SAUNDESRS INVITATION)

(MIKE VAX MY FOOLISH HEART)

(MAYNARD FERGUSON PLAYS "MAYNARD FERGUSON")

(MAYNARD FERGUSON GIVE IT ONE)

(ERIC MIYASHIRO GIVE IT ONE)

BIBLIOGRAPHY

La Revolución de la Inteligencia   Dr. Luis Alberto Machado

The Limits to Growth   Dennis H. Meadows

The pleasure to find out   Richard Feynman

Visions of Technology   Richard Rhodes

The Party is over   Richard Heinberg

The Third Chimpanzee   Jared Diamond

Listening to Jazz   Jerry Coker

Improvising Jazz   Jerry Coker

Shadows of Forgotten Ancestors   Carl Sagan & Ann Druyan

Ciencia y desarrollo: Douglas R. Hofstadter

Mayo/junio 1980/núm. 32/ año VI

Gödel, Escher, Bach Ofrenda

músico-lógica